T0348134

BWB Texts

Short books on big subjects
for Aotearoa New Zealand

Reconnecting Aotearoa

Loneliness and Connection in the Age of Social Distance

EDITED BY KATHY ERRINGTON AND HOLLY WALKER

Contents

Introduction

KATHY ERRINGTON

'We live in small worlds and big worlds at the
same time and we can't forget one or the other.'
– Kazuo Ishiguro

I chose a quote from Ishiguro above to open this book as I believe that he is the fiction writer who best captures how loneliness can warp our grip on reality.

This book looks at the connections between the 'small worlds' and 'big worlds' that pervade our lives. In particular, it looks at loneliness: how our world can be made to feel so much smaller, sometimes because of features of the 'big worlds' in which we live. Contributors explore the connection between the 'big' political contexts that surround us, and our 'small' private personal lives, and seek to explain how our worlds can be made small, or to seem small, by loneliness.

During my time as Executive Director of The Helen Clark Foundation I commissioned two reports into loneliness, and my co-editor Holly Walker led the subsequent research. These reports focused on data about who experiences loneliness in Aotearoa, and her chapter here recaps the major insights that she found.

Loneliness is defined in different ways by scholars working in different disciplines. It has been defined by some researchers as the gap between actual and desired meaningful social contact.[1] Other definitions emphasise an objective lack of meaningful and sustained communication. For example, the Duke Social Support Index asks participants questions such as: 'What is the number of times in the past week spent with someone not living with you?' and 'What is the number of times in the past week you talked with friends/relatives on the telephone?' These kinds of metrics are useful to policy-makers, and loneliness is increasingly being measured by governments, including those in New Zealand and the United Kingdom.

Loneliness research suggests there are three main types of loneliness: emotional (related to the lack or loss of an intimate other); social (feeling unconnected to a wider social network, such as friends, family and neighbours); and existential (related to a feeling of lacking meaning and purpose in life). Experiencing any one of these for extended periods has a similar damaging impact on health and wellbeing, but the solutions vary depending on the type of loneliness being experienced.[2]

In this text we wanted to focus more on how loneliness is experienced and felt than on the research data. The bulk of this book builds off Helen Clark Foundation research in order to explore how loneliness is experienced and what kinds of connections might ameliorate it.

Some chapters deal more specifically with loneliness than others. Some chapters address research on loneliness or the experience of that phenomenon specifically.

Others circle around loneliness, exploring related concepts like isolation, solitude and disconnection. The chapters also gesture towards antidotes to loneliness, such as cooperation, whanaungatanga, home and belonging.

This book does not claim to account for all loneliness experienced across time. As is clear from reading the chapters, the stories presented here reflect Aotearoa at a specific moment in time: in particular, addressing the effects of Covid lockdowns on this country and our society. And not every perspective on loneliness within Aotearoa is presented here. This book will have its blind spots and its gaps. The hope is that the conversation that this book opens, or continues, can be supplemented by further contributions in other forums.

The conversation begins with Holly Walker's report *Alone Together* in 2020. Holly used data from the General Social Survey 2018 to establish a pre-pandemic baseline of self-reported loneliness in Aotearoa, including identifying some of the groups most affected. She then drew on early data from the 'Life in Lockdown' survey by the Roy McKenzie Centre for the Study of Families and Children and the Institute for Governance and Policy Studies at Victoria University of Wellington (VUW) to sketch the early impact of the Level 4 lockdown on New Zealanders' self-reported loneliness. In Holly's 2021 update paper, she drew on quarterly wellbeing statistics gathered as part of the Household Labour Force Survey during 2020, as well as the VUW researchers' follow-up Level 1 survey, to provide a fuller picture of how New Zealanders' levels of loneliness were impacted by an extraordinary pandemic year.

The initial survey was undertaken during the third week of the lockdown, and asked respondents various questions about their emotional wellbeing, including how often they had felt lonely in the previous four weeks. About 11 per cent said they had felt lonely most or all of the time. By contrast, the equivalent figure in the 2018 survey was only 3.5 per cent. We owe a debt to Kate Prickett and her team for generously sharing this unpublished data with us in 2020. It made the scale of the problem obvious.

The Helen Clark Foundation analysis found that loneliness intersects in complex ways with other well-being factors: those more likely to experience chronic loneliness include people with low incomes, those who are unemployed, Māori, young people, disabled people and single parents. The mental and physical effects are significant – comparable to those of smoking and alcohol consumption. The impacts of social isolation teach us that we cannot deny the body's influence on the mind and vice versa. Simply put, loneliness is a significant and complex public health issue that must be urgently addressed.

While the Foundation's own research focused on Aotearoa, a growing body of literature internationally supports the need for social connection too. One striking study from Australia showed that people with better friend networks lived longer than those with few friends.[3] After controlling for a range of demographic, health and lifestyle variables, the study showed that networks with more friends helped to keep people alive during a ten-year follow-up period. A similar study in Sweden found that smoking and lack of social support were the two leading risk factors for heart disease in a group of middle-aged men.[4] It also found that having friends was a bigger protective factor than having a life partner or children. In part, this is explained by the fact that people with resources find it easier to make and sustain friendship. But this is not the full story. There is a physiological benefit to friendship too – fundamentally, friends make it easier to cope with stress. A study at the University of Virginia found that many people were put off by the prospect of climbing a steep hillside. But when people were climbing with a friend, researchers found they rated the hill as less difficult than those who were alone.[5]

This book does not aim to repeat or replicate existing research. It builds on that research, and offers a more exploratory approach to questions arising around loneliness. How is the relationship between poverty and loneliness manifested in contemporary Aotearoa? What are Māori perspectives on loneliness or related concepts? How can factors like age, disability, race, gender and class lead to challenges or variations in how loneliness is experienced in day-to-day life? This book poses these questions, and more, without purporting to provide definitive answers. It aims to start conversations rather than to close them down.

The following text is structured as follows; the essays transition over three areas, though all contributions have depth that cuts across the categories.

The opening chapters look at some of the background data, frameworks and concepts that can help to understand loneliness in Aotearoa today. Holly Walker opens by setting out what the data showed from the Helen Clark Foundation research projects, and what policy responses we recommended. Carrie Stoddart-Smith and Max Rashbrooke discuss the resources needed in order for people to lead less lonely lives, financial resources and whanaungatanga in particular, depending on where a person is situated.

The middle chapters have a more qualitative, experiential focus. They ask how loneliness and social (dis)connection are experienced. Susan Strongman discusses a moving account about her mother, Kiki Van Newtown about parenting a medically fragile child, and Athena Zhu about maintaining family connections across borders.

The final chapters draw on experience and background frameworks to pose questions about dealing with loneliness in the future. Gaayathri Nair discusses the complexity of digital connections, and Luke Fitzmaurice-Brown explores belonging, home, rangatiratanga and how the pandemic enabled new expressions of collective Māori identity and authority.

The public health restrictions during the Covid-19 pandemic, while necessary, made maintaining social connections much more difficult. Now that the immediate crisis has passed, this presents an opportunity. As painful and isolating as the pandemic has been, it has also thrown the importance of social connections into sharp relief, and highlighted where they have become fractured or non-existent. In doing so, it has provided an opportunity to repair them directly and purposefully.

In the final analysis, I hope that this collection can act as an intellectual springboard to push back on the myriad forces that separate us from each other, and a political call to action – in the 'big world' – to value the 'small' private worlds that we need to thrive. I am grateful to all of the contributors for helping us explore the different dimensions of this important conversation.

1. Very Different Boats

The Essential Policy Conundrum of Loneliness in the Age of Covid-19

HOLLY WALKER

When Aotearoa New Zealand went into lockdown for the first time in March 2020, I was a few weeks into a new job as the Deputy Director and WSP Fellow at The Helen Clark Foundation. I had been attracted to the role in part because of its flexibility; with a six-year-old and a two-year-old to parent, a PhD thesis to complete, and a partner to whom I hoped to at least wave occasionally, a largely self-directed role researching big public policy challenges seemed like a great option, especially because it could be done mostly from home – I didn't know then of course that soon we'd all be doing that.

Loneliness – and its causes, effects and public policy implications – was already on the table as a potential topic when Kathy, our director, and I sat down to sketch out the Foundation's 2020 research programme in February of that year. It had been suggested by our partners at WSP, whose international colleagues had been exploring interesting intersections between loneliness, transport policy and urban design. We agreed it was an important topic and set it down to return to in the second half of the year.

A few weeks later when the 'big world' drastically confined us all to our 'small worlds' in the first lockdown (something we didn't even know was possible before) loneliness soon began to feel like the *only* topic to usefully explore. 'Social isolation' had stopped being something you vaguely worried your elderly relatives might experience and was now apparently our primary public health objective. What would this mean for us all, for our mental and spiritual health, our social connections? How would this deeply unsettling experience change our communities – both in the immediate shock of it all, and over the longer term?

Now, from the comfortable distance of three years' hindsight, everything about those early months of 2020 has the eerie, half-remembered quality of a fever dream. The Foundation rapidly rearranged its research agenda. I paused the road safety report I had started work on – no one was driving anyway – and instead began researching loneliness and its implications in the few snatched hours each day in which I could work. Ironically, I was researching and writing about loneliness when I had never been less alone; each day I was physically barricading myself in a shed in my backyard to get enough space from my children to work. Kathy, meanwhile, was on brief parental leave after the birth of her second child but checking in regularly. Looking back, I'm honestly not sure how we did it but, by June, Kathy had returned to work and we had released *Alone Together: The Risks of Loneliness in Aotearoa New Zealand Following Covid-19 and How Public Policy Can Help*. The only way I can explain it is that it felt somehow *essential*.

Even then I was aware that we were all experiencing lockdown differently – people like Kathy and me were at home with our small children, trying desperately to carve out space to work or think, while others were going weeks without touching or speaking to another person. This was an important element of the problem – there was no 'one way' to be lonely in lockdown. Even though the public discourse at that time was all 'he waka eke noa' (all in the same waka) and 'team of five million', most of us were in fact in very different boats, and that sense of shared experience from the early 'be kind' days did not hold for long. The Covid-19 lockdowns were miserable for many people, but they were miserable in different ways for the sole parent caring for young children, than for the tertiary student away from home for the first time, than for the single disabled person without paid work. What all three had in common though, was a high risk of experiencing loneliness.

As the moving and diverse experiences related later in this book show, the causes of and solutions to loneliness are – in every case – bespoke. Yet its prevalence and impact are significant – and societal. How do we prescribe a public policy solution for that?

My aim with this chapter is to equip readers with a snapshot of what local and international scholarship and data on the topic reveal about the causes, prevalence and impacts of loneliness in Aotearoa New Zealand before, during and 'after' the pandemic. I hope to offer some ways of thinking about what this *means* that you can carry forward as you read and interpret the personal essays and issue-specific contributions that follow. This chapter draws extensively from *Alone Together* as well as our 2021 follow-up report, *Still Alone Together: How Loneliness Changed in Aotearoa New Zealand in 2020 and What It Means for Public Policy*, and updates them both where possible.

The first thing to say about loneliness is that it is of course a normal human experience – perhaps even an essential part of what makes us human. We've all felt it, and we all will feel it again. There are various ways to define it, but at its core, loneliness is the distressing feeling we experience when our needs for human connection go unmet. I like the formulation Kathy used in the introduction, which expresses loneliness as the gap between the level of connection we want, and the level of connection we actually have, because it nicely captures what an individual experience it is. Two people might have the exact same number of close relationships and social experiences, and while one might be perfectly comfortable, the other might be debilitatingly lonely. Numerous individual, cultural and socio-economic factors play a part in determining where we each fall on this spectrum.

As Kathy further outlined in the introduction, researchers have identified three main types of loneliness: **emotional loneliness**, related to the lack or loss of an intimate other; **social loneliness**, feeling unconnected to a wider social network; and **existential loneliness**, related to a feeling of lacking meaning and purpose in life. In their different ways, the contributors to this collection touch on all three. While the causes and solutions differ between these broad categories of loneliness, they each produce essentially the same emotional and physiological experience. Anyone who has experienced a particularly acute bout of loneliness – living alone for the first time perhaps, or following a relationship breakdown, since loneliness often correlates with moments of major life transition – will know why countless song lyrics and works of great literature serve it up to us in metaphors of physical pain. Very often, loneliness literally *hurts*.

There is a biological reason for this: humans evolved to live collectively and to rely on each other for survival. In ancient tribal societies (and today) other people ensure we have enough food, protection, warmth and care when we are weak or sick. Perceiving ourselves to be 'separated from the pack' triggers an automatic threat response in the brain, or what scientists call 'hyper-arousal' or 'hypervigilance'. It's the same 'fight, flight, or freeze' response triggered by any threat – useful when there is a genuine danger, but not a state we are designed to exist in for extended periods. Prolonged or chronic loneliness can therefore create hormonal imbalances, disrupt sleep, weaken our immune systems and increase our risk of various physical and mental health conditions, including high blood pressure, cardiovascular disease, high cholesterol, dementia, depression and anxiety. There is a large and well-documented body of research showing a direct link between chronic loneliness and reduced life expectancy. This is why loneliness is such a significant public health and policy challenge, as well as a challenging individual experience.

Of course, what I've just outlined is a very Pākehā, technocratic and Western science-based way to characterise this challenge, and I think it's important to acknowledge at this point that it is equally valid – indeed vital – to analyse these issues also as spiritual, emotional and cultural ones. There are plenty of Indigenous models and frameworks through which the role, function and importance of social and emotional connection can be viewed differently: via Tā Mason Durie's Te Whare Tapa Whā, for example, which conceptualises the components of Māori wellbeing as the four walls of a wharenui, or via the five ways of wellbeing model that conceives of mental health as a function of many social, physical and emotional factors, or via one of many culturally specific Pacific wellbeing models.[1] What the Foundation's public policy approach and all these others share is an understanding that connection – whether familial, social or cultural – is a fundamental and critical part of being human. When vital connections are severed, things can quickly go very badly wrong.

What we measure matters, and we are fortunate in Aotearoa New Zealand to have an official measure of loneliness as part of Stats NZ's wellbeing statistics, collected via the General Social Survey (GSS). Under non-pandemic circumstances, the GSS is undertaken every two years, and asks a representative sample of residents aged fifteen and older about a wide range of economic and social indicators, including how often they felt lonely in the four weeks prior to taking the survey.[2] Before the

Covid-19 pandemic, almost 40 per cent of respondents reported some feelings of loneliness during those four weeks. Some of these – 3.5 per cent – said they felt lonely *most or all of the time*. While this may be a small proportion of the total population, it is a lot of very lonely people when you consider that 3.5 per cent is just shy of 180,000 people. Interestingly, despite a quiet but insistent drumbeat of stories about a loneliness 'epidemic' even before the pandemic, in the three surveys preceding it (in 2014, 2016 and 2018), rates of self-reported loneliness in Aotearoa New Zealand were fairly stable.

Prior to 2020, the GSS was conducted in person, and interviewers were just about to head into the field to knock on doors when the first Covid-19 lockdown started. This left Stats NZ with a predicament worthy of Alanis Morissette: unable to conduct a survey about loneliness because everyone was in isolation. Fortunately, officials clearly realised if there was going to be one year to make sure to collect loneliness data, this was it, and quickly pivoted to include several GSS questions, including the loneliness measure, in the non-contact Household Labour Force Survey (HLFS). Better still, the HLFS is conducted quarterly, and can be broken down by more categories than the GSS. As a result, through the darkest days of the pandemic in 2020 and 2021, we had a rich and extremely timely series of regular, nuanced loneliness updates. I'm immensely grateful to these unnamed Stats NZ officials; this kind of dedication and creativity from public servants should be recognised and celebrated more often.

The stories that could be unpacked from the quarterly loneliness updates during the pandemic are as numerous and complex as the individuals surveyed, and the two reports we produced on the topic really only provide a bird's eye snapshot. This is partly why we decided to commission this collection of essays – to fill in the outlines of those reports with the colour, detail and emotion of individual lived experience. But even at headline level, the official data tells an important story about loneliness in Aotearoa New Zealand before, during and after the pandemic – and it isn't the one you might expect.

Asked to picture someone at risk of loneliness, many people think of an elderly person, living alone, perhaps unfamiliar with the digital technologies younger people use to stay in touch with their peers. But while some older people certainly do feel very lonely – as Susan Strongman's beautiful essay about her mum illustrates – older people are in fact the least likely age group to report feeling lonely. Statistically speaking, loneliness is very much a young person's game.

More than that though, data tells us that loneliness intersects significantly with other factors that materially affect people's wellbeing. As well as young people, those most likely to report feeling lonely most or all of the time include those on very low incomes or who are unemployed, sole parents, new migrants, Māori and disabled people. It's no coincidence that these are all groups who routinely experience marginalisation, discrimination and poor health, and who historically have often been the target of punitive and regressive policies. Many people will identify with more than one of these identities, and – as with other forms of disadvantage – intersecting risk factors can significantly compound the negative impacts.

During 2020 and 2021, as we moved past the shock of the initial lockdowns and the pandemic ground on, loneliness levels among the general population remained reasonably stable, but this finding largely masks the severity of the experience for those most affected. There was little change in *who* was most likely to feel lonely, but there were some quite alarming changes in *how many* people in these groups were reporting feeling lonely, and *how often*. We reported on some of the most confronting findings in *Still Alone Together* in 2021: while only 3.3 per cent of the general population said they felt lonely most or all of the time, almost 10 per cent of unemployed people felt this way. For the general population, the split of people who felt some loneliness versus none at all was about 40/60; for sole parents it was almost the other way around, with just under 56 per cent saying they felt lonely at least some of the time, and only 44 per cent that they never did.

We had a particular focus on disability in our second report, which found that a shocking 11 per cent of disabled people reported feeling lonely most or all of the time in the first year of the pandemic. When asked why she thought that might be, Prudence Walker, then chief executive of the Disabled Persons Assembly (DPA) New Zealand (now Kaihautū Tika Hauātanga Disability Rights Commissioner at the Human Rights Commission) said:

> There are so many things we need to have in place –
> or just to think about – in order to connect with people
> and it is exhausting. All of these factors mean that we

can feel excluded in many ways; this, I believe is a major contributing factor to loneliness.

I find Prudence's comment very telling – it's *exhausting* trying to connect with other people in a world that doesn't make that easy. In the examples Prudence went on to give for disabled people, it might be a lack of accessible transport preventing them from connecting with others, or the fact that the venue for a gathering they would like to attend is physically inaccessible, that information about a social club or society is not provided in a format that they can engage with, or that they can't fully participate in a community or family event because of a lack of NZSL interpretation. In an equitable society, individual disabled people would not be tasked with bridging the gap between the level of connection they want, and what they actually have; we would do this collectively by enacting policies that we know will help to create the conditions to allow these connections to thrive.

It strikes me that the same applies to all the groups revealed by the data to be most at risk: it's exhausting trying to connect with people when you're expected to first bridge a huge social or economic divide that others just don't face. For someone on a low income, the gap could be bridged by a guaranteed, liveable minimum income, so they could afford transport to catch up with a friend over coffee and could pay for their coffee – and maybe even shout their friend – when they got there. For a young person, it might be affordable internet access at home and school so they can connect with like-minded people online, along with responsible internet regulation so they are not at the same time exposed to disinformation, online bullying or harmful material. For a sole parent, it might be a combination of more affordable childcare and the opportunity to live in a warm, safe home in a neighbourhood that has been designed to facilitate social connection and opportunities for children to play. These are all public policy solutions to loneliness – something we traditionally see as a very individual problem.

The reports on loneliness I authored for The Helen Clark Foundation in 2020 and 2021 both concluded that – even without the pandemic, but especially in light of it – loneliness has such profound impacts on our people and communities that it is worth making a concerted public policy effort to tackle it head-on.

The challenge has not materially lessened since. While loneliness for the general population seems to have settled into something similar to pre-Covid-19 levels, the same groups remain at higher risk – and improvements in the way data is collected and reported are revealing more population groups to consider. After the lockdown prevented the GSS in 2020, Stats NZ managed to get it out in the field in 2021. The results were reported in 2022 – they're back to every two years now. While I still think quarterly would be preferable, they have thankfully retained some of the improvements from the HLFS, including the ability to break down the data by disability status, and added some new categories, like LGBT+. And guess what? While only 3.2 per cent of the general population said they felt lonely most or all of the time (which remember, is still 150,000-odd people), this rose to 7.2 per cent of LGBT+ people, 6.0 per cent of recent migrants, 6.5 per cent of young people aged 15–24, 5.7 per cent of sole parents and 9.9 per cent of disabled people – still, the worst affected.

As the chapters in the rest of this book show, the granular, personal and household solutions to loneliness will of course always vary according to culture, community, family, values, income, impairment and preference. That's as it should be, but it doesn't and shouldn't prevent us from making a concerted public policy effort to tackle it. This doesn't mean government or its proxies intervening ham-fistedly in people's lives to 'help' – indeed, when you read these essays, you'll find it impossible to imagine how that could be done in ways that aren't paternalistic, punitive or wrong-headed.

Rather, it means identifying the conditions that allow meaningful social connections to thrive, and investing time, money and political leadership to create and support these conditions. In *Alone Together* and *Still Alone Together*, we identified six planks of an effective policy response to loneliness from central government (noting they should all be developed and delivered in partnership with hapū and iwi, communities and local authorities). We still think these are the best place to start:

- Make sure people have enough money, by implementing an effective guaranteed minimum income for all New Zealanders to enable everyone to live with dignity;
- Close the digital divide, by making the provision

of high-speed internet access standard in all social housing tenancies and a standard feature of government-funded disability support programmes;

- Help communities do their magic, by investing in community-led development to support groups to realise self-identified collective goals;
- Create friendly streets and neighbourhoods, by prioritising social wellbeing and accessibility in all social housing developments and issuing guidance to stipulate that all urban development projects should promote social wellbeing and meet the highest standards of accessibility;
- Look out for people who are already lonely, by prioritising services and supports for those most at risk of experiencing loneliness, including young people, unemployed people, sole parents and disabled people; and finally,
- Invest in frontline *and* preventative mental health.

While not always directly policy-oriented, the essays that follow all illustrate the value of a policy response to loneliness. More than that, they elevate the conversation from the theoretical and technocratic real of government statistics and policy recommendations to the visceral and human – to meet loneliness where it lives.

2. Loneliness and Poverty

MAX RASHBROOKE

As other essays in this volume make clear, people may be lonely for all kinds of reasons. But because socialising, like so much human activity, often involves expenditure of some kind, a lack of resources can nonetheless be a central driver of loneliness. As documented in the Helen Clark Foundation's 2020 report *Alone Together*, low-income households are far more likely to report feeling lonely than their wealthier peers. Roughly one-quarter of people in households earning under $30,000 were lonely 'most', 'all' or 'some' of the time, and another quarter were lonely 'a little of the time'. Only half reported not feeling lonely. In households earning over $150,000, by contrast, roughly one-third felt lonely to some degree, while two-thirds did not.[1]

This relationship between loneliness and poverty is best understood in the context of long-running debates about what the latter concept truly means. For centuries, researchers have discussed whether poverty is essentially absolute or relative. Is it, in the former case, a matter of not having certain 'basic' things, of being deprived of material objects, of having a standard of living well below a fixed or 'absolute' marker? Or is it, conversely, about not having the things that other people have? Is being poor fundamentally a matter of having less relative to others? Is anything that limits people's ability to fully flourish also, somehow, a form of poverty?

In a developed society like New Zealand, the banal truth is that both kinds of poverty are real, and important. There is of course an 'absolutist core' of poverty, in the words of the Ministry of Social Development's Bryan Perry, whose semi-annual publication *Household Incomes in New Zealand* is the gold standard for inequality reporting.[2] Some people simply cannot afford basic items like heating, nutritious food and proper clothes for their children. Among the very poorest are the 102,000 New Zealanders living in 'severe housing deprivation'.[3]

However, even supposedly 'absolute' poverty turns out to have a relative dimension, as views change over time as to what constitutes a 'basic' material standard of living. A century ago, the absence of an indoor toilet might not have been held to constitute absolute poverty, because outside toilets were still widespread and not uniformly seen as a sign of deprivation. Today, indoor toilets are literally a legal essential. Even apparently 'absolute' standards are in fact relative.

Social Needs

Moreover, because humans are 'social as well as physical beings', in Perry's words, even a list of 'basic material needs' will include things like 'social engagement that involves financial cost'.[4] The connections between poverty and loneliness run deep, then, for there are many social situations from which people may be barred by lack of income. Some years back, a long-term homeless man, interviewed anonymously for Wellington magazine *FishHead*, recounted how he had been placed in city council housing in Northland, a suburb some distance from the CBD. But as none of his friends, who were generally as poor as he, could afford the bus fare to come visit, he had given up the flat, and had lived successively in an abandoned building, the service area of a multi-storey carpark, and a garage in the Aro Valley. Although evidently substandard, these dwellings had a proximity to the central city that allowed him much greater contact with his friends. In a world of relatively little social housing near city centres, poverty was forcing him to choose between social contact and adequate housing.[5] That he chose the former speaks volumes about sociability's importance to the human psyche, but also testifies to the barriers that poverty can place in the path of people seeking human warmth.

Such stories can be anchored with data from statistical surveys. In 2019, some 11 per cent of New Zealand children lived in families who reported being in 'material hardship' – that is, they were unable to afford six or more of the items deemed necessary for the 'minimum acceptable way of life' mentioned above. These items included 'a meal with meat, fish or chicken (or vegetarian equivalent) at least each second day' and 'two pairs of shoes in good repair and suitable for everyday use', but also 'suitable clothes for important or special occasions' and 'presents for family and friends on special occasions'.[6] The latter questions highlight the way in which poverty can limit social contact and thus increase loneliness. Another survey question asked how many respondents 'did without or cut back on trips to the shops or other local places'. Again, the figure was 11 per cent of the population; again, the isolating effects of poverty were pronounced.

Along similar lines, the 'Family 100' research project, undertaken some years ago by the Auckland City Mission, showed how the city's poorest individuals were often rendered lonelier by financial pressures. Families spoke 'of avoiding inviting friends over because they are unable to offer their guests anything to eat, and fear visitors might notice that their cupboards are bare … all too frequently families feel socially isolated and unable to participate in events that are important to them.'[7] The research noted the cultural dimensions to this exclusion. 'For families of Maori or Pacific heritage, there are certain expected contributions that can add further financial pressure, such as funerals, unveilings and birthdays; these can cause financial strain and further increase personal debt … the sense of shame and stigma at being unable to meet cultural obligations often results in people opting out of such events.'[8]

The 'unrelenting stress of food insecurity' and its 'destructive influence on the wider social networks' also made children more isolated, the research noted. Parents kept children home from school 'because they do not want to give their children food for lunch that singles them out as being poor. There is also hesitation about taking up free food programmes for the same reason.'[9] (The government's free school lunches, which go to all children at participating schools and were launched since the above research was carried out, may have changed this picture.)

These effects can be seen in individual stories. Community support worker and sole parent Tamara Baddeley, interviewed for the 2013 book *Inequality: A New Zealand Crisis*, described how her after-tax weekly income of $490 left almost no budget for anything other than essentials. She and her daughter had last gone to the movies four years previously when she won tickets off the radio, and had not had a holiday – other than visiting her parents in Taupō – in six years. If they went to watch the Hurricanes at the local rugby clubrooms, a $4 jug of lemonade had to last them through the evening. Extra income, Baddeley said, would make a substantial difference to her ability to socialise. 'I'd like to be able to know that if I wanted to go to the movies at the weekend, I could actually do it and enjoy it, and not have to figure out what's going to be cut to let me do that. Or I'd like to be able to plan for a real holiday and go somewhere where you're not relying on someone's hospitality ... Or go to the clubrooms and actually buy a beer rather than a jug of lemonade for four dollars ... Or maybe I could cut back and not have to work Sunday, and be able to go away for a weekend.'[10]

In addition to putting certain social interactions out of reach, poverty can also create intense levels of stress that themselves make socialising difficult. The Family 100 research found that debt was often an issue. 'The need to borrow from family and friends causes extra strain affecting family support systems,' the project's summary report noted. 'Balancing a budget that simply does not add up places extreme stress on partners and their relationships.'[11] Social interactions, if they raise questions as to whether a family's finances will be sufficient, can themselves be a source of stress. It is not always clear ahead of time how much expense will be involved in, for instance, going to a restaurant, especially if it cannot be predicted who will be ordering what and how the final bill will be allocated. Economic stress also has a wider impact on family functioning in ways that can constrain opportunities for social contact.[12]

A Corrosive Social Relation

The relative nature of poverty has another dimension, one that again connects to the question of loneliness. As far back as 1776, the seminal economist Adam Smith was pointing out that life's essentials included 'not only the commodities which are indispensably necessary for the support of life, but whatever the custom of the country renders it indecent for creditable people, even of the lowest order, to be without'.[13] The phrase 'the custom of the country' highlights again the relative element of poverty, the sense in which people are poor if they do not have what mainstream members of society possess and have determined to be necessities. Smith's insight is reflected in the standard global definition of poverty, used with variations in most major economies, in which hardship is described as 'exclusion from the minimum acceptable way of life (standard of living) in one's own society because of inadequate resources'.[14]

In this sense, poverty is closely connected to inequality, and is partly about being made to feel inferior in some way.

Poorer people may, as a consequence, feel inadequate in mainstream New Zealand social life, in part because they sense that they don't present themselves in the 'right' way or that others are looking down on their clothes, household items and other material goods. Interviewed for the 2021 book *Too Much Money*, Pete Bryant, a Wellington man who had been homeless much of his life, recalled: 'You get rich people that just look down on you like you're a nobody. They look at your appearance and the way you dress … I've spoken to a couple of rich people and they have looked right over my head, and thought nothing of it. They can't wait to get away from you, because you're not on their level.'[15] Along similar lines, British academic Ruth Lister has described poverty as 'a shameful and corrosive social relation' characterised by 'lack of voice; disrespect, humiliation and assault on dignity and self-esteem; shame and stigma; powerlessness, denial of rights and diminished citizenship'.[16] This dynamic can lead people to avoid certain social situations, and thus to feel lonely.

Public Perceptions

One final question is whether the public views poverty in this way – and whether, therefore, there is public support for tackling poverty's impact on loneliness. There is relatively little evidence on this question in New Zealand, but research from Britain – a country with reasonably similar political institutions and attitudes – is revealing. Surveys there show that, in the words of academics Stewart Lansley and Joanna Mack, '[p]eople perceive that needs extend beyond the basics of food and shelter; [they perceive] that poverty is dependent on the society in which they live'.[17]

In polling carried out last decade, Britons endorsed the idea that a list of necessities – things needed in order not to be classed as 'poor' – should include items enabling 'celebrations on special occasions' and 'a hobby or leisure activity'. Nine in ten respondents thought people were poor if they couldn't afford to visit friends and family in hospital, 78 per cent believed that being able to attend a wedding, funeral or similar occasion was a necessity, and 70 per cent said being able to afford a hobby was an essential part of not being poor.[18]

One of the most striking findings was that the more Britons debated poverty, and were exposed to others' opinions and given a chance to reflect deeply, the more generous their views became. In focus groups run by Lansley and Mack in 2012, participants' understanding of poverty 'tended to broaden spontaneously as discussion developed, moving from subsistence definitions focusing on deprivation or "basic" needs, to discussions of relative deprivation and its effects on social participation, social networks and support'. As one focus group participant put it, '[i]f a person hasn't got a vast or sufficient income then they can't participate in activities. They're excluded from communities, if you like.'[19] While such findings cannot simply be imported

34

from one country to another, it seems plausible that New Zealanders may likewise understand the connections between poverty and loneliness, and – if given the chance to discuss the issue in depth – support action to address both problems.

3. Whanaungatanga

A Foundational Value of Aotearoa

CARRIE STODDART-SMITH

Ngāpuhi, Ngāti Whātua

Introduction

There is a renowned whakataukī in te ao Māori that personifies the impact of a human loss when someone of importance departs this realm of being: 'Kua hinga he tōtara i te wao nui a Tāne' (A great tree has fallen in the forest of Tāne).

While traditionally offered for the passing of revered rangatira, today it is common for many whānau to adopt it in reference to their loved ones. Particularly, those who served as their place of shelter, security and sanctuary. For us, that was our dad.

When Dad took his last breath, I wasn't there despite my desperate efforts to never leave his side in his final days and weeks. With Covid lockdowns, I hadn't been able to travel to him as often as I'd hoped. As is natural with grieving, I continue to carry guilt for not being there more and being absent when his mauri moved from this realm to the next. I learned what it feels like for that tōtara to fall in the forest of your heart. I felt Rūaumoko (god of earthquakes) make his presence known, as I trembled with anger at myself for having left his side. I began to comprehend the great anguish that Ranginui (the sky father) and Papatūānuku (the earth mother) would have felt at their being separated for eternity. Although we had been saying goodbye in our own ways since his diagnosis, the final goodbye, we'll never get back. But whanaungatanga reminds me that we share an unbreakable bond. A bond that began before I was born and will continue after our deaths.

The Diagnosis

The whakapapa of my story begins before the coronavirus made its presence known globally. In October 2019, Dad began experiencing issues with his memory. After an urgent trip to the hospital, we learned he had a large brain tumour that had metastasised from his lungs. Without surgery, he would have died in a matter of weeks. He was diagnosed with stage four lung cancer. Our first course of action was creating a shared support arrangement. We moved Dad in with our sister immediately, and she would become his primary carer for his final years. It was intended that I'd fly home every six weeks to spend time with him and provide respite for my sister and her whānau. That couldn't happen.

On the positive side, surgery, chemotherapy and radiation treatment, together with his stubborn desire to beat the cancer, gave Dad almost three extra years on this Earth. Social distancing, household bubbles and improved community hygiene practices also helped in his recovery from his treatments and therefore the extension of his life. For him those extra years enabled him to live comfortably despite the toll his treatments would take on his body. But they also encompassed lost time together, and therefore the inability to properly process our imminent grief and for all of us to be actively present for his final years.

The Pandemic

In Aotearoa, we will collectively remember 23 March 2020, the date we would enter a state of national emergency and a series of lockdowns that would forcibly separate whānau. For those of us living in Tāmaki Makaurau that separation would last almost two years, and longer for those living overseas. Prior to the onset of the pandemic, I spent time with Dad in early March 2020. I wouldn't spend time with him in person again until December 2021. Living in the city where Covid lingered meant travel restrictions and heightened concerns about Covid transmission – especially as he was immunocompromised – prevented us from making the connections we yearned for as a whānau.

Understanding whanaungatanga
Whānau is the root word in whanaungatanga, referencing the centrality of kinship and familial bonds to Māori society. Relationships form the basis of all things in te ao Māori, from our creation stories through to our everyday way of life. However, like many people, I come from a mixed heritage background, being both Māori and Pākehā. Although there are stark differences in our ways

of knowing and being in both cultures, whānau is central to both my worlds. We predominantly grew up with our taha Pākehā (Pākehā side), but we were raised collectively through the efforts of our parents, our grandma, aunties, uncles and alongside our cousins – forging continuous and unbreakable bonds.

Its extension whanaunga refers more broadly to relatives or reciprocal relationships that don't necessarily have genealogical linkages. When we look to the Pacific and parts of Asia, we refer to those of the Austronesian linguistic family as our whanaunga – we are related through the migrations of languages.

Whanaungatanga weaves seamlessly between my worlds. It conveys the philosophy and practice of forging relationships through shared experiences and aspirations. Whanaungatanga relates to our connections with our whānau, our friends, to all those with whom we share a close and enduring relationship and to those we hope to forge connections with. It's personal, it's familial, and it's collective. It's built on manaakitanga – trust, respect, care and humility. Whanaungatanga is guided by rights and obligations that are sourced in our tikanga for the purpose of establishing unity and cohesion to advance the collective wellbeing. It is not only physical. It manifests in the infinite bonds between people as well as the places, memories and experiences they share.

In contemporary society, all three of these concepts have been broadened out beyond references to traditional kinship such as whānau, hapū and iwi to include kaupapa whānau (like-minded association of people) or rōpū (groups) organically developed to serve a collective set of goals, aspirations or a common purpose. Whanaungatanga finds resonance in various cultures around the world. In China an analogous concept is referred to as 'guānxi', while in Japan comparable notions are expressed in 'hedataru' and 'najimu' when forging personal relationships, and in 'shudan ishiki' that reflects group consciousness and harmony. Likewise, in the Philippines the practice of 'bayanihan' reflects the cultural emphasis on community cohesion and harmony, and in Malaysia the tradition of 'gotong royong' captures that same spirit.

Throughout the pandemic, we saw new modes of whanaungatanga take shape through increased use of digital communication platforms in a vast array of settings. This gave rise to new words, such as the 'zui', merging Zoom and hui, as part of our daily Covid lexicon. Digital platforms enabled whānau to overcome geographical separation and in some cases created a new normal involving more regular contact with whānau in different parts of the country and overseas. In some whānau, tangihanga (funerals) were livestreamed to enable members to grieve with each other and carry out their cultural duties from a distance, adapting our tikanga to manage this shift – although this wasn't without its challenges such as differing views on its cultural appropriateness. But while there was a level of novelty for some during those first few days or weeks of the unknown, many whānau were left stranded in their isolated realities without an internet connection, internet-capable devices, or awareness of and access to digital communications platforms.

As the world changes through more accessible connection points such as the development of new technologies, greater global mobility, and therefore increased multiculturalism within societies, new forms of kinship, relationships and connecting with each other will naturally emerge. In response, our conceptions of whanaungatanga continue to evolve and adapt, evidenced through the growing body of wellbeing frameworks and re-conceptualisations of tikanga Māori across our community-level organisations and within our national policy architecture. Those threads continue to stretch further out to weave across health, economic, social and environmental sectors in the public and private domains. The resurgence of wellbeing as an indicator of our nation's progress appears to have amplified this socio-cultural shift driven by the government's Living Standards Framework as a core determinant of its policy decisions. However, the onset of Covid meant many of us were not mentally or emotionally prepared. We hadn't fully comprehended the impact that policy-enforced constraints on our physical connections would have on our ability to develop shared experiences – and what that would manifest as – during a time when those connections were most needed. A time that will indelibly shape the world's history and its future.

Preparing for the Future

In reflecting on what we could do better if a similar situation arises, the key is preparation. The likelihood of another global pandemic or crisis is inevitable. Preparing mentally and emotionally will be critical to navigating any rapid changes and social shocks. It's important then that the government and our broader public sector think beyond the tax take and economic measures alone in our future policy settings, and look more creatively at areas that will have a greater impact on social cohesion. Without relitigating almost two centuries of government-mandated policy inequity, a stronger and more cohesive nation will emerge through greater investment in mātauranga Māori and the cultural institutions from which that knowledge and knowing is sourced. For Māori and indeed other cultures, enhancing mental and emotional wellbeing and preparing for the future will not be met through a narrowly Westernised health focus or by targeting the economic recovery alone.

Our tīpuna developed strategies over thousands of generations to care for our whare tapa whā (four cornerstones of Māori wellbeing) in the face of prolonged separation and disconnection due to navigating and exploring vast areas of ocean to discover and settle new lands. These strategies seek to consistently find ways to nurture our wairua (spiritual wellbeing), hinengaro (mental wellbeing), tinana (physical bodies) and whānau (family and relationships) and were especially important during these isolating activities. Sharing and embodying those wisdoms is essential for the social and cultural uplift of Aotearoa.

In this space, there is a growing desire from whānau for Māori-led and government-enabled investment to support stronger connections to our whakapapa, language and knowledge systems – both in knowing and being. This dialogue goes beyond free te reo classes or workshops in the workplace. It moves more deeply into the metaphysical or spiritual realms. Where better knowledge and understanding of cultural rituals like karakia and mōteatea (traditional chants) help us manage our emotions and connect us to our atua (gods). It advances the need for the right infrastructure to be in place to support existing and build new cultural learning institutions, to invest in digital technology that supports the development of intimate connections and cultural confidence across generations and within and between cultures.

Investing in and supporting alternative ways to enable people to develop their wairuatanga (spirituality) in culturally appropriate settings will provide them and their whānau with the tools to maintain their mental and spiritual strength through periods of crises. Because when we can begin the work of mastering our tools, we are better positioned to fulfil rather than perform our cultural duties. Investing in cultural development and practice is essential to effectively develop modern ways of transmitting, receiving and evolving the mātauranga that has been handed down from our tīpuna. Much of that mātauranga is tied to our language and its various dialects, to our various rohe (regions), and to the lived and imagined experiences of and by our tīpuna. Practicing our culture doesn't require us to be the expert in it, but it does give us the confidence to embody or adapt our tīpuna tools to help us adjust and remain steadfast during those times we feel lost, alone or emotionally challenged.

These can be big and small acts of practice. One of the small ways that I maintain my connection to Dad is to remember him weekly on a Wednesday evening – the anniversary of his passing – in the way that we were most at ease with each other: over a quiet drink with our quiet but connected thoughts and dreams for the future.

Whilst the focus of this story has been on a mixed Māori–Pākehā experience, it's equally important to ensure that the cultural knowledges and institutions of the many diverse peoples who have come to call Aotearoa home are also better resourced, supported and enabled through government policy and investment. This must be an and/and not an either/or approach. Aotearoa was founded and built on values that emerge through whanaungatanga. When we strengthen whanaungatanga and our concepts of whanaungatanga through investing in cultural identity and belonging, we create opportunities for our relationships to flourish domestically and internationally and pave the way for a radically inclusive society. When our cultures are strong and cohesive, when our values and aspirations are mutually beneficial, and when our environment is sustainably supporting all of us, only then can we co-design and co-decide the best possible future that is capable of withstanding the many challenges that we will undoubtedly face going forward together.

Moe mai ra e te pāpā

4. Loss of Incidental Connections

SUSAN STRONGMAN

When Mum called to say her garage flooded, I drove down to Hamilton to help clean up.

When I arrived, I found boxes of books, clothes, paintings and drawings, some close to fifty years old, from when my sisters and I were kids, lying in shallow puddles of murky water that had leaked in through the walls and roof. Sodden on the concrete floor lay an ancient suitcase, brought from Scotland when my grandparents emigrated, filled with papers and letters and photos and documents.

Mum keeps everything. She likes to surround herself with objects – like an external brain made up of hundreds of tangible items that elicit memories and hold meaning. These items – often referred to as 'memory objects' – line her cupboards and drawers and pile up in the garage.[1]

The external brain's epicentre is the fridge. It's plastered with photos of her university friends, cats and dogs long dead, kindergarten classes she once taught, her brothers, daughters, granddaughters, nieces and nephews, and of unidentified children of friends' children's children.

From the fridge, the memory objects creep through the house like ivy – drawings, postcards, vases, plates and newspaper clippings. Her parents' lounge suite, ceramics clumsily moulded by kids' fat little fingers, a framed picture that I drew aged five, bags stuffed with crumbling sprigs of lavender and carefully folded baby clothes – hers, my sisters' and mine. They shoot down the hallway, into the bathroom, the bedroom, even the toilet (here lives a newspaper clipping about Hadrian's Wall, a world map and an old concert flyer).

I call it clutter, dusty and chaotic. But almost everything in the house holds meaning for Mum, and I suspect these objects evoke fond memories for her, helping to fend off the loneliness that can creep into her life.

Humans are social animals, so experiencing long periods of loneliness can severely impact on our physical and mental health – leaving us prone to anxiety and depression and increasing our risk of things like dementia and heart disease.

Mum ticks a lot of the boxes that put her at risk of loneliness. For most of her adult life she worked as a teacher – a busy, exhausting, badly paid job. It was a stretch for a solo parent of a shitty teenager (me), but she was surrounded by people – friends, colleagues, kids, parents and caregivers. For Mum, teaching was more than a job, it was a social network. It held meaning and gave her purpose, it was part of her identity.

Research tells us there are many factors, those afore-mentioned boxes that Mum ticks, that can contribute to loneliness. In 2018, some of the people most likely to feel lonely were unemployed. Though Mum's actually retired, it's not really by choice. Does that make her unemployed? No one is stopping her from applying

46

for jobs, but her skill set is limited to little outside of wrangling pre-schoolers, which requires a certain level of energy, I'm told. It's also harder for older people – especially women – to enter or re-enter the workforce.[2] To me, Mum's always been old. She was forty when I was born, much older than my friends' mums. Now she's seventy-seven, and I'm thirty-nine – about to start a family. We are both young at heart.

Another factor that can up the risk of loneliness is having a low income. The 2022 *New Zealand Retirement Expenditure Guidelines* suggest that for people living outside of Auckland, Wellington or Christchurch, $650.34 is the weekly amount required to achieve a basic standard of living that includes few, if any, luxuries.[3]

Mum's annual income, after tax, is $33,103, or $636.60 a week. She pays $450 a week for the rental where she lives with her memory objects and her two cats. It can be lovely there. When the sun's out, she sits on the deck and reads a library book or sends extraordinarily long text messages to friends and family. In summer, she leaves the sliding doors open all day and grows flowers and vegetables in pots. She mows a little patch of grass, but lets weeds grow high in the garden beds, where the cats make nests to snooze in the shade.

It's far better than the last place she lived – a boarding house with antisocial, often aggressive housemates and neighbours, usually with piles of stinking rubbish in the shared kitchen. (Living in boarding houses is an increasing trend among older women, who are less likely to be chosen as employees or flatmates.)[4] But it's also more expensive and the rent keeps going up.

In winter it's cold, and damp. Mould grows on her clothes and shoes and the bathroom ceiling. Sometimes water comes in through the walls, and the carpet gets musty. Often from her bedroom at night, she can hear people in the flats across the road shouting and screaming, which keeps her awake.

She used to be friends with her neighbours – the nice man upstairs and the couple next door. Having them around made her feel safe. Often the couple would drop by with a meal, a loaf of homemade bread, or oranges off their tree. She'd repay them with a cup of tea, lemons off her own tree or fresh fish from my sister. They all kept an eye on her. But when the neighbours' flats sold, and the rent went up, they all moved out. They keep in touch, but I know Mum misses having them right there.

Anxiety about money also keeps her awake at night. After rent, Mum has $186.60 a week to spend on things like power, food, petrol and insurance. Though many people in Aotearoa make do with far less, things are tight for Mum. It's painful to see her struggle, to visit her at home and find a near-empty fridge.

She's taken to reusing tea bags and pocketing instant coffee sachets whenever she gets the chance. In winter, despite the biting Hamilton cold, she keeps the doors and windows open most of the day to air out the house, only turning the heater on after dark. To further save power, she showers only every few days, and cooks all her food in the microwave.

There is a pervasive and toxic stress that comes with being broke. For Mum, debt is a constant worry, as are her living conditions, the wellbeing of her family and the cost of healthcare. At her last visit to the dentist, to have several teeth pulled out, she went without sedation to reduce the cost.

Being broke can also hinder the formation and maintenance of relationships. The large group of old friends she used to see so often – the ones in the photos on the fridge – she sees less of now. Without an income, she can't make the journey out of town to visit, can't afford to split the bill at lunches or trips out to dinner. She wouldn't dream of ever saying that though – instead, she avoids their calls and emails, and makes excuses not to go. Other things that once brought Mum pleasure, like seeing a movie or having a glass of red wine, are off limits now too.

Just being around others is a significant salve for Mum, and she is not alone in that: in the UK, a survey found that 33 per cent of respondents deliberately caught the bus in order to have some human contact. For Mum, it's people in cafes, rather than bus passengers, who keep her company. Most days she will go to a cafe – often McDonald's, where her SuperGold card means she can get a $2 flat white. Surrounded by people, she sits for hours, reading the paper, sending those long texts punctuated with cat and flower emojis, writing cards and letters to friends that, more often than not, she doesn't get around to sending.

But in March 2020, when the country went into lockdown, the cafes all shut. It was a particularly hard time for Mum. At first my sisters and I worried that she'd go stir-crazy and refuse to stay home. But in fact she avoided leaving the house, even for walks, so the only human contact she had was with my sister and niece (who live in Hamilton), when they dropped off groceries and sat in the asphalt driveway for a physically distanced cup of tea.

During lockdown, while many people stayed in touch with friends and family more than ever before, the bad cellphone reception and lack of internet connection at Mum's meant calls would drop out or not even go through and video calling was not even an option. (Fortunately, this did not affect Mum's ability to send her text messages.)

It's not uncommon for people over seventy-five to not have internet at home. Others who tend to lack access are people living in social housing, unemployed people and those living with a disability.[5] In *Alone Together*, The Helen Clark Foundation reported that people on low incomes can find the experience of loneliness particularly challenging because they often lack access to the material and social resources to buffer its negative effects, such as high-speed internet, warm comfortable homes and access to plentiful food:

During and after the Covid-19 crisis, affordable internet access has become even more important to enable people to retain social connections. There was already a strong case that a suitable device with an affordable internet connection should be considered part of the baseline for social inclusion, in the same way that a landline with free local calling was a baseline last century; in the post-Covid-19 environment this is even more important.[6]

In early 2021, a new job with a higher salary and more flexibility meant I could set up and pay for an internet connection at Mum's place and work some days each week from her home.[7] Mum can now make voice and video calls to her heart's delight, though texting remains her preferred method of communication.

While loneliness tends to decrease with age, evidence both in Aotearoa and overseas suggests it begins to increase again once people reach seventy-five. In line with this, in 2020, people aged over seventy-five were the second most likely group to feel lonely most or all of the time (after eighteen to twenty-four-year-olds.)

Since we know that poverty intersects with loneliness, it is alarming, but perhaps not surprising, to learn that in Australia, older women are the fastest-growing group in poverty. There are numerous factors that contribute to this. Like many women, Mum arrived in retirement without a partner, sufficient savings (thanks to the gender pay gap and the tendency for women to work less because of caring duties), or a home.[8]

While home ownership is in decline across all age groups, housing is more precarious for low-income older women (especially Māori and Pasifika women), and renters are more likely to live alone with lower annual incomes, and with poorer health. As is Mum's experience, renters are vulnerable to increasing costs of tenancy, and must also live with the risk of having to move out at any time.

Which brings me back to the flooded garage.

In order to save money, Mum had cancelled her contents insurance. Many of the damaged items were irreplaceable – it was the memories these things evoke that are priceless to her. Mum and I spent a nice few days together, going through these boxes of memories together, saving what we could, throwing out what we couldn't.

My sisters and I have finally convinced Mum to join a waitlist for pensioner housing in Hamilton. The units look nice, warm and community focused, with plenty of space for her memories to spread.

5. On Isolation and Connection when Parenting a Medically Fragile Child

KIKI VAN NEWTOWN

Pandemic life has been a prism of overlapping and opposing experiences. I don't know how to reconcile the two deeply incongruent layers that I look back on, but when I do sit and reflect on the last few years it feels like trying to sew patches onto dissolving blankets. Each stitch lands to the side of where I intend, compromising the strength of the weave. Instead of thick, warm spans of fabric, I end up producing little knotted bundles of softly broken fibres that look like tiny haystacks.

The looking back feels sore. I suppose that's why my brain invokes metaphors as a kind of psychic cotton wool, a protective mechanism to stop my mind zeroing in on the unequivocal truth of the last three years. If I think too hard it makes me feel like I'm peeling, a fallen log in a forest, slowly breaking down in a pattern and structure of decomposition perfected over billions of years. I feel small and inconsequential and tired.

———

When Covid hit in March 2020 I had already been dealing with an epidemic for a year. Most people don't remember but during 2019 there was a measles outbreak across Aotearoa. Over twelve months several thousand cases sprang up with increasing regularity. Two people miscarried pregnancies due to infection. In October the outbreak was transported to Sāmoa, where seventy-nine people died, the majority of whom were babies and small children.

While most people didn't experience any impacts from this epidemic, it completely restructured how my family organised our lives for most of the year. Measles is incredibly infectious. It's estimated that if one person has it, 90 per cent of people around them who are not immune will catch it. It lingers on surfaces and stays in the air for hours. For immune-compromised people, the chance of surviving a measles infection is 50/50.

During spring, when cases were really starting to increase and spread across Aotearoa, I shared multiple updates on Facebook:

2 September 2019:

Hello friends! I'm feeling really terribly scared about this measles outbreak because the people I love who are immune-deficient could die if they are exposed. I know we've all got a lot on, but if you can please prioritise getting your MMR booster – it'll take 30 minutes at your GP and it's free!!

And thirty days later ...

2 October 2019:

Cool cool cool guess we're never going to anything ever
again

The kids didn't go back to most of their activities for
the rest of the year, and we spent the summer assessing
very carefully where we could go and what we could do
to minimise our risk of exposure to measles. Managing
disability and chronic illness is constantly demanding
that your wellbeing matters in the face of ambivalence.
Being disabled and chronically ill is being acutely aware
of how eugenics continues to bloom through legislation,
policy and the everyday ways in which we relate to each
other.

———

The first layer I can try and describe is my own personal
internal experience, which has been full of expansive
hope, freedom and a calm and clarity that I had previously
only ever caught in glimpses – launching off a rope swing
into a creek as a kid, running downhill through the bush,
standing alone on the edge of the Welsh coast, laying like
a cornice between the plains of life and death.

I lived in Ōtepoti in my early twenties, up on City Rise.
Around the corner on Rattray Street was my friend's
house, a small brick and white bungalow with well-worn
carpet and heating. For his birthday one year we built a
fort in his lounge, stacking up furniture and using brooms
to create apexes in the sheets and blankets. We stayed in

there all night, six or seven of us, nestled in sleeping bags and around the couch legs, passing around whiskey and weed and candy and chips. Together we'd built a nest, and that small enclosure felt safe, slow, and eventually as we slept, still. We hibernated together overnight, but I would've been happy for it to last a whole season.

When we first went into lockdown this is where I went. To joyful containment. To small walks and a little life. My pulse rerouted my ordinarily frenetic thoughts, and I felt firm on the ground for the first time in a long time. I planned. I did exceptional work. All of the extraneous parts of day-to-day life had been excised and I was able to communicate intentionally, with less regard to social norms and the management of other people's expectations and emotions. It was completely liberating.

I released an album in May, and instead of playing shows we held a series of twelve Personal Parties with friends and fans, convening over Skype to play a few songs, talk about justice, do tarot readings, and chat about community and mutual aid. These are some of my favourite gigs of my whole musical career, tiny miniatures, intimate and detailed, covering the expanse of distance, and diving right into what it means to be alive.

While most people were lamenting the loss of public 'third spaces', us neurodivergents and introverts were celebrating this recalibration of what social life is supposed to look like. The renovation of digital platforms for connecting and collaborating opened up a precedent for accessibility that I hadn't previously experienced. Staying home removed the debilitating hubbub of the commute, the workplace, the bar. It reduced the whiplash that exists between the public contortion of trying to move through an unaccommodating world, and the private exhaustion that inevitably follows.

———

My family went into lockdown a few weeks ahead of everyone else in mid-March. I'd been tracking infection numbers through February, and we'd begun making preparations to go into isolation. While shipping crates around the world were being repurposed for makeshift hospitals and refrigerated morgues, we were gathering tinned foods and flour, and getting vegetable seedlings in the ground. I became a prepper, talking friends through the steps they could take to get organised – refresh your water tanks, make sure your gas bottles are full, stock up on Panadol and ibuprofen.

During this time one of my employers incredulously said they hoped I wasn't panicking, and then explained that it wouldn't be tenable for me to continue my contract if I had to work remotely. This one interaction was transcribed over and over across the world as corporations and politicians scurried to downplay the seriousness of what was coming. The denial was messy, and the suggestion of changing the status quo even temporarily was seen by many as absurd.

Those of us already operating in the margins watched a game of tug-of-war play out from the sidelines, as political leaders and billionaires desperately gripped onto the rope, straining against each other with faces like red balloons. But behind the theatrics, beyond left and right, both teams remained firmly committed to the belief that collateral damage is a natural feature of progress. And in the end it was always just number crunching to figure out how many body bags a society would tolerate.

This violent truth was readily apparent to those of us never invited to join a team in the first place. And so without a rope to grab hold of we fell back on the gentle hands of our communities to shelter us from the dark. We assembled together in group chats and on Zoom, rolling our eyes and sharing memes, and asking 'how are you doing?', which is code for 'I'm here for you, I love you exactly as you are'.

———

The second layer is more like a tidal wave at the door. It was the public experience all around me – my family, neighbourhood and community, the team of five million, and billions more scared souls across the world. It was loud and crashing, bringing with it debris that could wipe a whole village out. We were lucky here because our leaders understood that during a catastrophe what people want is calm and firm boundaries, exceptional communication, regular programming to tune in to and some collective laughs. But as the weeks turned into months turned into years, the noise became crueller, more obscene. A waning enthusiasm for public health measures became eugenics lite, which in turn burgeoned into full-on fascism. A neighbour whose kids had been a regular fixture on our trampoline before the pandemic started posting articles about natural selection.

There has been a great grief going around which is antithetical to my own experiences. Initially it was the mourning of 'normality', which is hard to sympathise with when you've never been privy to normality in the first place. It was the loss of public life where people could have their existences witnessed, and this landed like a bombshell to those used to defining themselves through the lens of others. All around me friends and colleagues and family were breaking down, and I was the king brat, swanning about in my trackpants and dressing gown, absolutely thriving in a crisis. Finally I was getting some of the solitude I have always felt homesick for.

———

When George Floyd was murdered by police in Minneapolis, the whole world seemed to explode into a revolution. Black Lives Matter rallied people together in the fight for racial justice, and in the protest marches and behind the makeshift shields other injustices were talked about too. This movement became a site for people to start locating and articulating the intersections of systemic oppressions – and disability and ableism joined the conversation.

Suddenly people were thinking about accessibility. Protesters diligently wore masks, event advertising had information about stairs, webinars sprung up in place of face-to-face meetings. Our daily Covid updates had sign language interpreters. We had been plunged into the largest mass disabling event the world had seen in generations, and this visibilising of disability made it politically necessary to consider access needs, and normalised doing so. For a brief window of time it felt like an open and accommodating and just world was easily within reach. And then it all evaporated.

———

Despite the fact that almost everyone will be disabled at some point in their lives, society teaches us to fear disability. Disabled people are seen as an existential threat, a constant reminder of the temporal nature of the human lifespan. And so through intentional design we are mainly kept hidden, sidelined, our lives cropped and corralled by carefully written policy, our invitation into public life and third spaces always offered with caveats. We are asked to navigate a world of constant and arbitrary barriers quietly, while the very architecture of space and construction of social norms are designed to discourage our participation.

For decades disability justice had by and large been left off the agenda of public discourse, but as soon as Covid hit all attention turned to the disabled community, where leaders and advocates were asked to guide plans and provide education on how to respond to the pandemic. The insights disabled people had honed over years in order to protect their own wellbeing – while navigating unending social and political obstacles – was suddenly respected expertise. At the same time, the existence of disabled people was scrutinised and debated in covert and overt ways by politicians, policymakers and anyone with an internet connection. Fiscal analysis took place, pitting the economy against disabled people's lives. This is another kind of whiplash all too familiar for those navigating an ableist world, where the value placed on our skills is contingent on the benefit it produces for the status quo, where our right to exist is transmuted into our productivity under capitalism.

———

The times I have felt most happy and free in my life have all been characterised by solitude, anonymity, social quietness. Once, long ago, I worked as a 'house girl' to a very wealthy elderly couple in Wales. I would spend my mornings working in the kitchen, delivering pots of tea to the library, ironing and running errands, before heading off to explore the nearby villages. One afternoon I found myself winding my way up the Great Orme in Llandudno. This giant ancient hill arches up and out into the sea from the north coast of Wales, and halfway around its peninsula the mainland disappears from sight. Up the top is a Victorian church and cemetery, and as I sat there on that overcast day with wind flurries blowing straight through my thin yellow jacket, I felt completely happy and content. Alone, silent, unwitnessed.

———

Throughout the first lockdown the bare roads were like emptied out arteries, and there was a great drawing-in of breath as we all waited to see what would happen. Would we be revived, would new blood flow through our veins, would we rise from the dead, and as what? Over the coming months we saw the kind of mutual aid flourish which is essential for a just world. We saw government money spilling into social care. There was suddenly accommodation for our rough-sleeping and houseless people, food parcels and an expansion of access to financial assistance.

Our society changed overnight as we stayed home, set up on Zoom in kitchens, bedrooms and laundries across the motu. We all became novice epidemiologists, and there was wide support for the evidence-based responses we took together. We celebrated our essential workers, and shared outrage at their minimum wage incomes. For a window of time many of us got to step out of the grind and into a space of possibility, where we could imagine what other futures might be possible.

This would be a chance for us to untangle what community really, truly means. To parse apart and honestly explore the limits of connection under capitalism, and to acknowledge how neoliberalism is reflected in the transactional ways we are taught to relate. For many of us, being apart and isolated was the greatest show of support and solidarity we'd ever experienced, and I remember during these slow, quiet and delicious months hoping so much that we would never go back.

And then we did. With Covid now circulating throughout Aotearoa, the government removed all public health protections to allow us to 'get back to normal'. And so my family, and many, many people I love, are back staying home, declining invitations, wearing masks and RAT testing on an almost daily basis. Seclusion and exclusion pinning us to the margins once more.

The difference this time is that we've seen how things can change when there is political will. The veil has disintegrated and we can now look directly across the threshold and point to what is possible. The idea of social care and a world reoriented away from capitalism is entirely within our reach, and we know this because we've quite literally just done it. And so while politicians and CEOs are demanding people get back to the office, disabled advocates and activists are also returning to business as usual – advocating for an accessible and just world for everyone.

———

There's a secret tree in my neighbourhood, where all the monarch butterflies go to wait out the winter. From one of the strong boughs is a long rope swing which moves in wide ellipses above the grass and dirt. If you stretch out and lean back you can see flowers and globe artichokes spilling from the nearby garden, and at the right time of year, if you glance back up you can see the butterflies begin to reemerge from the branches.

6. Love in the Time of Covid

ATHENA ZHU

It's 7.04 a.m. on a clear autumn day. Dawn is approaching and the first rays of sunlight are beginning to seep through the forest canopy. I'm surprised by how good I feel despite having only had three hours' sleep.

Hiding behind a tree, I wait excitedly for our guests to arrive. Fourteen sleepy people have gotten up at the crack of dawn to witness Colin and me exchange our wedding vows. It's the intimate, unconventional, somewhat bizarre wedding set in nature that I've always dreamed of.

What I'd never dreamed of was that I would get married on the other side of the world with none of my birth family present. Nor had I imagined I would marry someone who had never been to my homeland or met my family in person. I thought that type of thing occurred in a different time, during the earlier settler period maybe, when a journey home took months on a boat.

This is 2021 and it seems that Covid-19 has granted us time-travel powers whilst stripping us of air-travel ones.

Colin and I met a year before Covid. He an American, me a Kiwi, both of us expats in China.

Like many Kiwis, I grew up dreaming of that great rite of passage, the OE. Although my plan was initially quite conservative – a hop across the ditch to Melbourne for a few years – my OE eventually extended over twelve years and counting. Riding the currents of economic forces, I drifted north from Australia towards Malaysia, Singapore, eventually landing in China.

That's how, in the age of modern air travel, telecommunications and multinational corporations, I became an expat. I've been in discussions over the years on what the difference is between an expat and an immigrant, if there even is a difference. From my vantage point as the child of immigrants, there is. Defining characteristics of expathood include more frequent cross-country moves, a greater familiarity with the annual work visa renewal process and an aversion towards owning any furniture. Most significantly, an expat has a different sense of identity and home, for the present and the future. Home has always been Aotearoa and I had never considered setting down real roots anywhere else (although I did crack a bit by the eighth year and adopted a dog).

On my last trip home before Covid, I hadn't brought Colin with me. We'd coupled up two months prior and in the transient world of expat dating, it had felt too early to invite him on the trip. As I climbed up Mount Tauhara one weekend with a book of nature-inspired poetry by Mary Oliver that Colin had gifted me, I regretted that decision. I yearned to share the feeling of my homeland with him. I hoped that one day soon he'd be able to compare the pine forests of North Carolina with the kauri forests of Northland, and revel in the beauty of our homes together.

Our relationship deepened over the following months and we started taking these trips. I joined him on his annual migration home to Chapel Hill and celebrated a winter Christmas, still a rarity for me. New Zealand was next. We booked flights to Auckland and hut spots along the Lake Waikaremoana track for February 2020.

I remember the moment that was the beginning of the pandemic for me. It was 23 January, two days before Chinese New Year. I had been on a business trip in Beijing and was about to catch the high-speed train back to Shanghai. During the three-day trip, there were murmurings of a novel virus outbreak in Wuhan. My colleagues handed me a mask before I left for the train station. I took it out of courtesy, thinking I probably wouldn't need it. But I did. Everyone on the train wore a mask throughout the five-hour journey. I saw no signs or official announcements about mask-wearing. It's amazing how quickly humans follow a crowd.

Over the next few days, the official announcements came and the larger ramifications of a world in pandemic started to unfold. Announcements of lockdowns in Wuhan, school closures and office closures. Shanghai usually gets quiet around Chinese New Year, but this was different. On the streets, every hour was 3 a.m.

A week and a half before our scheduled flight to Auckland, we were on our way to lunch at a friend's when Trump announced travel restrictions from China into the United States. Colin asked me if New Zealand might do the same thing. 'No way!', I said as I ignorantly suspected Trump's move was driven by factors unrelated to actual epidemiological logic. I knew so little and had so much to learn.

We did decide that evening though to shift our flights forward, realising there was no point in waiting around in a ghost town. Somewhat arbitrarily, we decided to reschedule to 3 February, the day after our next friend gathering (nurturing your 'friendmily' is critical to expat survival).

As it turned out, that wasn't quite early enough. Around noon China time on 2 February, New Zealand announced the closure of borders to non-residents travelling from China, starting at midnight. Our flight was scheduled to depart at 00.05.

We still went to the airport together, but only one of us boarded the plane. This time, the pain of Colin's absence was much greater. I had by then pretty much figured out that he could be my partner for life, but it felt impossible to make that decision without him meeting my family and my homeland. Can he really commit to being with me without seeing the people and the place that made me? I felt like this scuppered trip was costing me the ability to progress in my relationship and my life. In despair, I resented the virus, and I resented national borders.

I stayed home for close to a month. We celebrated Mum's sixtieth birthday, took a trip to Taupō Bay and Cape Rēinga, and watched Covid unfold throughout the world. At the end of the month, I started thinking about returning to China. It was extra hard to leave home this time, there was so much uncertainty. How severe would this virus be? How long will it last? What will happen if it hits New Zealand? What if my family catch it? However, I had a sense that China might change their entry rules and if I didn't go back soon, I might not be able to. I didn't want to leave Colin, or the business I was building there, in limbo. At the beginning of March

I returned to Shanghai via an eerily quiet transit through Hong Kong airport.

My prediction become a reality. China and New Zealand became two of the very few Covid-free havens in 2020 due to the restrictive travel policies they enacted. During the tough moments of missing each other, my family and I found relief that we were in the two safest countries on Earth.

The unprecedented travel restrictions tipped the rules and calculus of expat lifestyles upside down. Gone was the security that you could go home whenever you want. Forget about using your location of work as a jumping-off point to travel the region. The trade-off of career progression and international experience at the cost of a little less family time had to be recalculated. Every expat has a Covid horror story. In mid-2021, I met a man at Shanghai Pudong airport who was on his way back to Spain. He was walking away from an exciting senior role at an industry-leading company where he had dedicated years of his life. Securing this position was originally a triumph, but that was before he had to grapple with the uncertainty of Covid travel rules, resulting in an unplanned separation from his toddler and wife for more than twelve months, with no end in sight.

For me, my trip home turned out to be the last time I would see my family in person for over two years, and the last time that I would ever see my grandmother. I was cycling home when Mum called from Grandma's bedside at Auckland Hospital. I stopped on the side of the road, cars and bicycles of Shanghai traffic streamed past me as I tried to tell my grandma 'I love you' one more time.

I had watched her slowly slip away over the past decade from Alzheimer's, so at least this wasn't a shock. Yet still, prior to Covid I'd assumed I'm only a flight away should anything happen, and I had deemed that a reasonable trade-off for the adventures of living abroad.

I lay awake that night waiting for the final phone call. It came around 3 a.m. Colin held me as I cried. I was so grateful then that at least I had the ability to talk to them, to see them even, although through a screen. Immigrants of the past wouldn't have had this luxury.

Covid made me acutely aware of nationality and citizenship rights, and the physical distance from family. I've heard that many other Kiwis have come to a similar realisation; I saw the media report that swaths of us had repatriated home. Covid has forced us to be conscious of how we choose our home; we can't be in the middle, one foot in, one foot out. Maybe that's a good thing. We are made to commit, to embrace the place we are in and people we are with more fully. But, as an economy with a small domestic market that needs strong exports to thrive, the loss of the Kiwi expat community may weaken New Zealand's cross-market knowledge, relationships and competitive advantage. Of course, less global mobility also means loss of the personal growth and learning opportunities that come from living abroad. These things are never simple to judge.

Throughout the two years, Colin and I frequently deliberated over whether or not to travel home. The rules meant spending up to five weeks in quarantine, quite challenging for us as entrepreneurs. More importantly, our circumstances meant we were each barred from entry to the other's home nation. Given the fluidity of rule changes, we didn't want to risk potentially being stuck apart, as we saw happen to several of our friends. After weathering Covid together, we knew for sure we were the dream team, but as foreigners, we couldn't get the paperwork to seal the deal in China. We watched intently for any indication of the rules loosening.

Finally, in October 2021, the press started reporting that the US was preparing to open its borders to travellers from China. As soon as the official announcement was released, we took action. Flights were booked, rings were made and we planned our wedding in two weeks. On the day we booked our flights, I managed to get to the fabric market thirty minutes before closing time to get a dress made. I was nervous when I told my mum our plans; we knew it would be unlikely for my family to attend due to the isolation and quarantine policies in New Zealand. She was hugely supportive and understood completely.

We tried to make the most of it. Since it wasn't possible to be traditional anyway, we let our imaginations fly. We held our ceremony at sunrise, outside in the woods. Colin and I hid before we approached the 'altar' together: I squeezed behind a tree, he lay prone in the grass. A close Kiwi friend who lived in Vancouver got ordained to be our celebrant. During our breakfast reception, Colin's family took turns reading out the well wishes sent by my family and friends in New Zealand. Our photographer, a former photojournalist from Turkey who had also been stuck away from family due to Covid, told us he had never heard of a dawn wedding before we called him and thanked us for the unique and memorable experience.

I was finally able to bring Colin home in 2022, although we were almost caught on the wrong side of the tracks again. Less than a week before our scheduled flight to Auckland, the Shanghai government announced a four-day lockdown that would end the day we were due to fly. Not willing to risk another season stuck away from home, we purchased a new set of flights and departed Shanghai the day before it went into what would actually become a two-month-long lockdown.

As the plane approached Auckland, I craned my head from my middle aisle seat, desperate for a first glimpse of home. I felt elated, relieved, joyous and safe, knowing I would soon be with my family and friends in Aotearoa. As soon as we could, we paid a visit to Grandma and introduced her to her newest family member. Gazing out at the Waitematā Harbour from her final resting place, holding Colin's hand in mine, I'm grateful that Covid has made me more sensitive to the physical distances from important people and places in my life, more appreciative of every moment I get to spend in their presence.

7. Digital Connection and Disconnection

GAAYATHRI NAIR

Over the last decade, due to the advent of smartphones, our lives have increasingly involved switching seamlessly between digital and physical space in moment-to-moment shifts. In one moment, we are having coffee with a friend, in the next they have gone to the bathroom and we are scrolling our Instagram feed or checking messages. In this time, digital connection to each other has been touted both as the answer to and source of loneliness. Digital connection has allowed people to look outside their physical communities for connection in a way that has never been possible before. At the same time, the ways in which relating to one another on the internet, particularly social media, drive loneliness are well documented. Our everyday face-to-face interactions with other human beings have declined dramatically since the youth of our grandparents and parents and as a result our relationships have increased in quantity but decreased in depth. This might sound dramatic but think about the last time you actually spoke to someone like a bank teller face to face or went through a supermarket checkout that was staffed by a human being.

These micro-social interactions matter, both in terms of our individual wellbeing, because they are the small things that make us feel like we are a part of a community rather than a single entity floating in space, and also in terms of building the skills we need to forge meaningful social connections in the rest of our lives. For example, it becomes much more challenging to strike up a conversation with a stranger at a party if you have never actually made small talk with a stranger before.

As a culture we are fascinated with the role of the internet and how the time we spend there affects us. Think pieces about everything from the rise of the Instagram selfie to the polarising nature of the YouTube algorithm abound. The evidence tells us that, ironically, while the internet has opened us up to exposure to the vast diversity of values, viewpoints and types of people that exist in the world, it has also meant that if we want to, we can find the specific people who are most like us and never stray outside of the comfort of that bubble unless absolutely necessary. This is reinforced by algorithms and targeted advertising that are invested in only showing us more of what we want to see so that we will spend more time on these platforms and therefore earn the corporations that built them more money.

It was not till the pandemic were we able to look at what it means to do so much of our significant human connecting through a digital medium. It is important to recognise the difference between loneliness and social isolation; loneliness.org.nz describes this distinction: 'Social isolation is where you do not interact socially with others; whereas loneliness is an emotional state that arises from not having the desired sufficient meaningful connections with others.'[1]

In Aotearoa, loneliness is highest amongst people aged 15–24. To be fair this is a segment of the population that has always struggled with disconnection and loneliness – adolescence is a difficult time and when we are trying to find our place in the world and in our relationships – however, this segment of our population is also our digital natives who have access to connection in ways never possible to this extent before, and yet it does not seem to assuage loneliness meaningfully. This falls into place when we look at how social media and other types of superficial digital connection affect our psyches. Scrolling through Instagram is like looking at a highlight reel of the lives of everyone you know. It becomes hard not to feel like your life is lacking, that you are missing out on meaningful connections that it appears everyone else is privy to. The evidence indicates that if we are able to use these platforms as tools by which we forge real connections that we take into our offline worlds, then they make us less lonely. However, if we use them as a substitute, a way of filling our time without having to put the effort into interacting with people outside of these platforms, then they start a vicious cycle of loneliness, where the act makes us feel lonely and we scroll more to avoid feelings of loneliness which subsequently serves to make us more lonely in the long term.[2]

The pandemic brought to light the immense potential and significant limitations of digital social connection on a scale and in a way we have never seen previously. What would it mean to only be able to see our close connections if we had the capacity to video call them? How would it affect us to have to actively avoid the everyday micro-social interactions we have with people for fear of the virus? As lockdown progressed people appeared to be adapting rapidly and finding ways of making it work. Zoom drinks, game nights and parties became ubiquitous; the team of five million became adept at keeping each other safe by moving our close personal interactions with each other into the digital space.

This was simultaneously valuable and disheartening to many members of the disabled community in our country. As things moved online, they became far more accessible to people with chronic illness and physical impairments, however, it shone a light on how much was possible but had not been done because currently able-bodied people did not feel a need and perhaps prioritised face-to-face connection over accessibility. It is important when we speak out the complexities of connecting through digital means that we do not neglect the fact that for some people, digital connection is the only way they are able to access any kind of meaningful connection at all, whether this be due to health, well-being or geographic isolation. Whatever the limitations of human connection in the digital space, it is still an important means of connecting and one that needs to continue to be explored and improved.

While digital connection allows us to connect with more ease than ever before – for example, time zones aside, my friend in Sweden is as accessible to me as my friends in Auckland or Australia – what the pandemic showed us is that it is not the same as face-to-face connection and cannot be treated as a replacement for it. While we may not always want to admit it, something is lost when our primary way of communicating is through the screen. There are many reasons for this; the tight framing in video calls is very different from how we interact naturally. It means we do not have access to the same volume of non-verbal communication as we do during face-to-face interactions. This means we must work harder to communicate basic things such as openness, warmth and interest, and we have to work harder to notice it. The intense eye contact of video calling is also not how we interact in the wild and can be immensely fatiguing. As the pandemic progressed people noticed how much more tiring it was to interact with people primarily in digital space due to this increased cognitive load. The term 'Zoom fatigue' was coined to describe this phenomenon.[3]

An additional complexity is that much of how we are able to connect in digital space is mediated by corporations who are driven by profit, which is reflected in ways that are sometimes unexpected. For example, as corporations are driven by getting better at getting us to buy things, they are focused on showing us only things that we want to see or, at the opposite end of the spectrum, stimulate a strong emotional response in us. As we spent more and more time connecting digitally our psyches were subject to these forces in more intense ways than ever before. We are only now beginning to understand what this means as our society fractures and polarises in unprecedented ways.

My own experience practicing as a counsellor during the pandemic was an exercise in understanding the value and limitations of connection through digital means. When lockdown began in March 2020, I was starting a new role. I had never delivered counselling through a digital medium before, and the learning curve was steep. I remember being shocked to find myself stress sweating through my clothing after each session despite not really doing anything different from how I had before. I noticed how much more draining I found each session compared to face-to-face counselling, feeling exhausted at the end of each day despite seeing a much lower volume of clients than I had before. This really spoke to the increased cognitive load that comes with trying to do work that requires an emotional connection with another person through this medium. Factors that I hadn't considered that I found affecting my practice: having my own image on the screen was distracting, and sometimes made it hard to give the client the same level of undivided focus I am able to during face-to-face sessions; similarly, being unable to prevent messages coming through from other people on my video conferencing platform – a small notification would pop up on my screen, and this changed the way I was able to pay attention.

I think this is true in general when we are connecting in digital spaces; we are almost always doing something else at the same time, and while it often doesn't feel like it in the moment, this has a significant impact on the quality of our interactions with other people. Whenever we are online our attention is almost always divided because in that world our attention is currency. One of my key skills as a counsellor is my ability to give the client one hundred per cent of my attention for the fifty minutes they are with me. I am not thinking about other things I have to do or rehearsing what I will say next; I am able to be fully present with them in the moment, something some of my clients have never experienced from someone before. I do not find it as possible to be this way in the digital environment because the mediums are not designed for me to be able to pay this kind of close attention and have this kind of presence with people.

As the pandemic progressed, I left that role and moved to being a counsellor in private practice doing a mixture of ACC, EAP and private work. During each lockdown I would experience a steep drop-off in client numbers, particularly from my regular clients. Somewhat counter to my expectations, I thought that loneliness and isolation would mean that my ACC clients would want to maintain connection to counselling at all costs, but that turned out to be the opposite of what happened. The reasons were somewhat varied, some people did not have a space in their home they felt was private enough, but for many it was because they felt that online counselling was deficient in some way and wanted to wait till they could come back to 'real counselling'. It remains true that despite the convenience of online counselling the vast majority of my clients prefer face-to-face appointments unless it is absolutely unavoidable.

All of this is not to say that relationships that exist primarily or completely in digital spaces are not meaningful or significant, just that they are different from relationships that exist primarily in physical space or across both dimensions and have limitations as all relationships have limitations based on a myriad of factors. Digital connection is an important avenue of connection to many people and helps to mitigate social isolation. However, I think the pandemic taught us how important meaningful face-to-face connection is and while we can live without it, it becomes challenging to truly thrive. The power of the digital is that it has opened up new ways of connecting for us, but simultaneously it cannot replace completely our old ways of doing things.

8. He Uri Ahau nō Te Aupōuri

LUKE FITZMAURICE-BROWN

During the window in which we pretended the pandemic was over, I headed north, ostensibly under the guise of research. He uri ahau nō Te Aupōuri, I am a descendant of Te Aupōuri, an iwi of the Far North, but for most of my life I have not really known what that means. Growing up I always knew I was Māori (or 'part Māori', as I called it then). It was never a source of shame, but it was never a source of pride either. But as an adult I wanted to know more, as thousands of us who have been disconnected from our whakapapa eventually do. Tentatively I began my journey home.

The first time I visited my marae I didn't know what I was supposed to do. I knew the tikanga of pōwhiri, at least in theory. I knew there were certain kawa, certain rules, for welcoming strangers. But who was I? Was I a stranger? Or was I of this place? Who was I to decide that? The tikanga for me that day was a scoop of ice cream from the shop next door. I stood outside the marae, ice cream in hand, and just watched. With my partner and two of our friends beside me, I tried to soak it all in. A familiar name on the nearby war memorial was a concrete symbol that I was in the right place. But mostly I remember how quiet it was. Reconnection that day was unassuming. Reconnection that day was the taste of orange chocolate chip.

My trip north this time was part of a piece of research into the Covid-19 checkpoints that were established during the first lockdown. The project was aimed at examining the checkpoints across the country as a case study in the expression of rangatiratanga for the iwi involved. It was an opportunity for me to learn more about the tikanga of rangatiratanga, and an attempt to give voice to a group of people who had taken extraordinary measures in a time of crisis. I wanted to know how it felt for people to come together under such unique circumstances. Was this a planned effort to assert rangatiratanga, or was it more spontaneous? Did checkpoint organisers think about it that way, or were other labels more appropriate? Or no labels at all? These were the questions that drove my journey north, at least as far as the work was concerned.

But on a personal level, the research was also an excuse to go home. I remember the enthusiastic reaction from my supervisor when I pitched the idea of a project based in my tūrangawaewae. 'That's the kaupapa,' she said, 'that's what this is all about.' Rightly or wrongly, I felt like I needed an excuse to show up. Perhaps that's a neoliberal imposition, surely we shouldn't need work or research as an excuse to visit somewhere we're told we belong? Or maybe that's just human. Either way, I had found my excuse.

It's tempting to romanticise some of these processes but in truth reconnecting with my whakapapa has often felt awkward. Not knowing what to do, not knowing who to speak to, not wanting to offend anyone – the journey sometimes feels fraught with risk. The fear of rejection is ever present, who am I to assume I will be welcomed back several generations after my family last called this place home? There is embarrassment in trying to return to a place without knowing why your family left, or what damage that did, or what that was like for those who remained.

There is also shame. There is a hesitance in choosing to return home in ways my family were never able to. I grew up thinking I was 'part Māori' because my family told me I was. I grew up not knowing my marae because I wasn't told what it was called. I may never know how many of those choices were deliberate and how many were inadvertent. But the subtext of reconnecting with my whakapapa is acknowledging the fact that my own family have inevitably played a role in keeping it hidden. I don't for a moment begrudge them that; colonisation visits terrible, invisible choices upon all of us. But my biggest fear is that my steps to reconnect will bring shame or embarrassment to the people I care about. My nana grew up in a time when it was shameful to be Māori, and sometimes it feels selfish of me to be revisiting that history. Maybe I am better to let sleeping dogs lie.

Or perhaps I am better to follow my nose and awkwardly stumble through, saying that I belong until someone else says it back to me. I was nervous about conducting the interview for our Covid research project, but in the end it was the kind of unremarkable process I had been through many times before. I spoke with one of the checkpoint organisers about what the lockdown was like from his perspective. Rather than talking specifically about rangatiratanga, he spoke of a sense of just 'stepping up'. It wasn't about protest or opposition; it was about doing what was needed to keep people safe. Nevertheless, it was deeply grounded in tikanga. The mandate for the checkpoints came from whakapapa and whanaunga- tanga, no further justification was needed.

During the interview, I was asked who my whānau were and I recited the list I had memorised, ringing through the maiden names in my matriarchal line until they eventually started to click. When connecting with people from my iwi I typically have to go back three or four generations until the whānau names start to register. My Māori whakapapa comes through the women in our family, and I sometimes wonder what my experience of reconnection would have been like had they not been forced to change their surnames with every new genera- tion. I inherited an Irish name through the men in my family, and nobody has ever questioned my Irishness.

'Actually, don't write this next bit down,' my interview subject said at one point. It was a fleeting moment, about an uncontroversial piece of information, but I felt like I had been let in on a secret. I had been deemed worthy of being told something not to be shared. It was a moment so fleeting that you might not have even noticed it, but moments of validation are never really minor. For a second, I was in. The significance of that wasn't lost on me. But for the most part, the interview was as unceremonious as that first visit to my marae had been. We spoke about the toll the checkpoints had taken on those involved, and the cost of staying on the front line

day after day. We also spoke about the immense reward –
those involved knew they were doing the right thing, and
their convictions proved to be well founded. But in many
ways our conversation was unremarkable. There was no
pōwhiri, no grand performance of welcome. It proceeded,
as all good things do, over a cup of tea.

Maybe that's one of the things that colonisation has
taken from us – the privilege of living as though we simply
belong. Before it described us as an ethnic group, the word
'māori' just meant 'normal'. It described (and continues
to describe) things which were ordinary. Our whakapapa
and our sense of belonging could be taken for granted.
Being Māori meant being māori. Perhaps that's still true,
but it doesn't always feel that way for those of us who
have been disconnected.

To know our whakapapa is our right as Māori, but that
also comes with responsibilities. There's a huge privilege
to being able to travel to a marae a thousand kilometres
from home. There's privilege in being able to reconnect in
the way I have tried to do. Some of us whose families left
our iwi rohe were never able to go back, and for some of
those who stayed there was an enormous cost to keeping
the home fires burning. There's privilege in my position
as a male, and as someone with light skin; I have never
faced the racism that most of my whanaunga have faced.
I have never experienced the racism that tauiwi of colour
continue to face in Aotearoa – sometimes it feels that as a
nation we are so determined to find ourselves biculturally
that we forget the struggles of communities who don't
fit the Māori/Pākehā binary. This is something I have to
remind myself of frequently. In my new-found zeal to

reconnect with my whakapapa, it can be easy to forget how much harder it can be for others to do the same. Finding a balance between enthusiastic embrace of my whakapapa and respectfully acknowledging the privilege of that often feels tricky and uncertain.

But there are moments that make the uncertainty all worthwhile. In 2018 my sister graduated from medical school, and as part of the Māori graduation ceremony it was my job to briefly speak in te reo on behalf of our family. I tried to whaikōrero as best as I could, then as a whānau we sung a waiata, as a gesture of how proud we all were. Afterwards my nana said to me that my great-grandmother, her mother, would have been proud of me. That too was a gesture, less performative, but for me, more memorable. I never knew my great-grandmother, but I knew how much it meant for my nana to say those words. I was proud of myself too, and proud of her.

On the final day of my research trip, the person I interviewed invited me to join him as he took a group of school kids out to the whenua. I felt like a kid myself, listening wide-eyed as he explained the whakapapa of the land. Afterwards he introduced me to a kuia from another iwi who was leading the group from the school. 'This is Luke,' he said with a grin, 'he's one of us.' She looked surprised, and for a moment my heart sank. But without missing a beat he said, 'Yep, we Aupōuris come in all shapes and sizes.' It was another moment so fleeting that it might barely have registered for someone else, but for me it was enormous. A few years after taking the first tentative steps towards reclaiming my whakapapa, it had claimed me back.

My whakapapa journey still feels tentative. It still feels tenuous and conditional. But it also feels mine. Two years on, that moment of being claimed feels as real and as important as it did the day it happened. I try to call the Far North 'home' now, as much because I want to practice saying it out loud as anything else. But I'm starting to believe it. Recently someone scoffed when I told them I was 'from' the Far North despite never having lived there, and their reaction surprised me. It made me realise how much I have internalised a whakapapa-centric understanding of where I'm from, and where I belong. In much the same way that the Covid checkpoints differed in the forms they took and the terms that were used to describe them, I have become comfortable with the idea that reconnecting with our whakapapa can look vastly different for each of us, and that's okay. Moana Jackson used to say that you can't be half a mokopuna, and I have finally begun to internalise that idea. I haven't described myself as 'part Māori' for years, and I try to gently correct anyone who describes themselves that way. He Māori koe, I try to remind them, sometimes as a way to remind myself as well.

Moana Jackson also used to say that whakapapa is a series of never-ending beginnings. Six months after my interview up north, my son was born. My hope for him is that he will walk proudly in two worlds, unencumbered by the challenges his parents faced, or his grandparents, or his great-grandparents. I'm sure he will face his own challenges, but I hope he will do so comfortable in the knowledge of his tūrangawaewae. I hope he will know that there will always be a place for him to stand, and a whenua which he is connected to. He will not need an excuse to travel home, and he will never describe himself as 'part' anything. He will be both Māori and māori, knowing that those connections are just a natural part of who he is. He Māori koe, I will remind him, again to be met with a look of surprise, as if that was ever in doubt.

Conclusion

KATHY ERRINGTON

This book aimed to connect the loneliness research done by The Helen Clark Foundation, outlined at the outset of the collection by Holly Walker, to more personal, experiential accounts, hopefully providing a richer picture of loneliness when taken together. The chapters are a sketch of loneliness in Aotearoa over the Covid-19 pandemic, but they are only a starting point. There is further research needed into how to facilitate face-to-face contact, and other issues raised in the book.

But more talk about loneliness is valuable on its own. It can help us to feel less ashamed, which might lessen our feelings of loneliness in the process. Over time, a sense of shared experience and responsibility can also build generosity, which Max Rashbrooke describes in his early chapter.

Generosity may be an important part of reconnection. Luke Fitzmaurice-Brown's chapter in particular articulates the power of small acts of kindness in making us feel connected. The intense feeling of connectedness Luke describes after the small gestures he experienced in Northland is moving in itself, as is the broader picture he paints of a united community. Here, the crisis of the pandemic allowed for a new collective expression of

Māori identity, and left Luke more comfortable in the knowledge of and connection to his tūrangawaewae. Carrie Stoddart-Smith and Luke Fitzmaurice-Brown's chapters both address the harms of disconnection from whakapapa, and describe the value of cultural connection as one way to feel part of a community rather than a single entity 'floating in space', as Gaayathri Nair describes it.

The chapter by Kiki Van Newtown about the complexities of parenting a medically fragile child complicates the privileging of face-to-face contact from the perspective of disability rights. Face-to-face interactions can be dangerous and exhausting despite their greater ability to make us feel connected.

Max Rashbrooke, Gaayathri Nair and Susan Strongman's chapters reinforce that there is policy work to be done on the value of resources for addressing loneliness and poverty. These resources can be financial, such as income support, emotional, such as counselling, or they can be cultural, as described by Carrie Stoddart-Smith and Athena Zhu.

All the contributors seek to raise these questions, and more, without purporting to know all the definitive solutions.

Reflecting her pedigree as a journalist, Susan Strongman's chapter begins with a compelling personal account. Knowing as I do that human stories are more compelling than data, I return to it now in the conclusion.

In late 2022, Susan's mother was hospitalised with a sudden and severe increase in blood pressure. The stroke-like symptoms she suffered caused blurred vision, dizziness, memory loss and confusion. After four nights under the care of a team of dedicated, hard-working and highly empathetic staff at Waikato Hospital, she was sent home.

It is important to state that the cause of this stroke is anything but clear. But the experience for Susan's mum – both disorienting and terrifying – offers a glimpse of the benefits of social connection: the kindness of a young woman in the next bed over sharing strawberries, the calming presence of a visiting friend, the seemingly endless capacity of nurses to share knowledge and provide comfort and reassurance.

After she was discharged, Susan describes taking her mum to an unfamiliar pharmacy for a blood pressure check. Stressed and anxious about change, her first reading was high. For close to ten minutes the pharmacist sat in a room and listened as Susan's mum spoke, about her fears and concerns, and life in general, before taking a second and third reading. Again it's impossible to pinpoint what caused her blood pressure to drop in this time, but the next two readings were significantly lower. Susan's mum now regularly visits the pharmacist, Denise, not just for blood pressure checks, but for the reassurance and familiarity that comes with a trusted social connection.

There is no single policy solution that will secure better social connection, but improved social connection is the right aspiration. Social (re)connection appears to be one thing that will address or at least ameliorate loneliness, even if loneliness is a more complex phenomenon that often also arises out of cultural positioning, particular life circumstances, and other factors. The chapters raise questions about how action to address structures of colonisation, gender, and class could help to address loneliness. There is room for more research on this in the New Zealand context, as well as more work on how isolated digital employment may contribute to loneliness.

I hope that this is the vision we can take from this book and the essays it contains. We should be hopeful and aspirational for what social connection can offer us, while simultaneously hesitant to offer universal prescriptions for how to address it. I finish writing this as New Zealand heads into an election year – changes are ahead for the 'big worlds' I alluded to in the introduction, that have major impacts on our own 'small' private lives.

Much has occurred in the period between writing that beginning and this ending. Whatever government takes office, my hope is that the benefits of social connection can be valued, nurtured and cultivated going forward. This will look different in different contexts. This book has sketched where future policy research could focus: addressing poverty, cultural alienation, digital connection and the accessibility of public spaces, among other areas.

At an individual level, while I do not believe any one person can change the systemic causes of loneliness on their own, I do hope that more discussion about loneliness can help lift the shame and stigma around what is a universal part of the human experience. There is no shame in being lonely.

Jean-Louis Guez de Balzac may have put it best (in a line attributed to him): 'Solitude is fine, but you need someone to tell that solitude is fine.'[1]

Notes

Introduction

1   For example, Samia C. Akhter-Khan, Matthew Prina, Gloria
     Hoi-Yan Wong, Rosie Mayston and Leon Li, 'Understanding and
     Addressing Older Adults' Loneliness: The Social Relationship
     Expectations Framework', *Perspectives on Psychological Science*,
     18, 4 (2023), pp.762–77.
2   Holly Walker, *Alone Together: The Risks of Loneliness in Aotearoa
     New Zealand Following Covid-19 and How Public Policy Can Help*,
     The Helen Clark Foundation, Auckland, 2020.
3   Lynne C. Giles, Gary F.V. Glonek, Mary A. Luszcz and Gary R.
     Andrews, 'Effect of Social Networks on 10 Year Survival in Very
     Old Australians: The Australian Longitudinal Study of Aging',
     Journal of Epidemiology and Community Health, 59, 7 (2005),
     pp.574–79.
4   K. Orth-Gomér, A. Rosengren and L. Wilhelmsen, 'Lack of Social
     Support and Incidence of Coronary Heart Disease in Middle-
     aged Swedish Men', *Psychosomatic Medicine*, 55, 1 (1993),
     pp.37–43.
5   Simone Schnall, Kent D. Harber, Jeanine K. Stefanucci and
     Dennis R. Proffitt, 'Social Support and the Perception of
     Geographical Slant', *Journal of Experimental Social Psychology*,
     44, 5 (2008), pp.1246–55.

1. Very Different Boats

1   Mental Health Foundation, 'Five Ways to Wellbeing', https://
     mentalhealth.org.nz/five-ways-to-wellbeing (accessed
     22 August 2023); Health Promotion Forum of New Zealand,
     'Pacific Health Models', https://hpfnz.org.nz/pacific-health-
     promotion/pacific-health-models (accessed 22 August 2023).
2   Stats NZ, 'General Social Survey (GSS)', https://datainfoplus.
     stats.govt.nz/Item/nz.govt.stats/2ed50ad6-8ab8-47df-883d-
     210a51b50043 (accessed 22 August 2023).

2. Loneliness and Poverty

1   Holly Walker, *Alone Together: The Risks of Loneliness in Aotearoa*

New Zealand Following Covid-19 and How Public Policy Can Help,
The Helen Clark Foundation, Auckland, 2020, p.16.

2   Bryan Perry, *Household Incomes in New Zealand: Trends in Indicators of Inequality and Hardship*, Ministry of Social Development, Wellington, 2019, p.111.

3   Ministry of Housing and Urban Development, '2018 Severe Housing Deprivation Estimate', https://www.hud.govt.nz/stats-and-insights/2018-severe-housing-deprivation-estimate (accessed 27 November 2022).

4   Perry, *Household Incomes in New Zealand*, pp.111–12.

5   Max Rashbrooke, 'In Shadows and behind Closed Doors', *FishHead*, August 2012, pp.34–38.

6   Bryan Perry, *Child Poverty in New Zealand: Trends in Indicators of Inequality and Hardship*, Ministry of Social Development, Wellington, 2022, pp.9, 30.

7   Emily Garden et al., *Speaking for Ourselves: The Truth about What Keeps People in Poverty from Those Who Live It*, Auckland City Mission, Auckland, 2014, p.31.

8   Ibid., p.5.

9   Ibid., p.31.

10   Max Rashbrooke (ed.), *Inequality: A New Zealand Crisis*, Bridget Williams Books, Wellington, 2013, p.88.

11   Garden et al., *Speaking for Ourselves*, p.31.

12   See, for instance: Jess Berentson-Shaw and Gareth Morgan, *Pennies from Heaven: Why Cash Works Best to Ensure All Children Thrive*, Public Interest Publishing, Wellington, 2017.

13   Quoted in Max Rashbrooke, *Too Much Money: How Wealth Disparities Are Unbalancing Aotearoa New Zealand*, Bridget Williams Books, Wellington, 2021, p.107.

14   Perry, *Child Poverty in New Zealand*, p.4.

15   Quoted in Rashbrooke, *Too Much Money*, p.29.

16   Quoted in Perry, *Household Incomes in New Zealand*, p.112.

17   Stewart Lansley and Joanna Mack, *Breadline Britain: The Rise of Mass Poverty*, Oneworld Publications, London, 2015, p.24.

18   Ibid., pp.18–21.

19   Ibid., p.24.

4. Loss of Incidental Connections

1   Sabine Marschall, '"Memory Objects": Material Objects and Memories of Home in the Context of Intra-African Mobility', *Journal of Material Culture*, 24, 3 (2019), pp.253–69.

2   M. Claire Dale and Susan St John, *Women and Retirement in a Post COVID-19 World*, Retirement Policy and Research Centre, Business School, University of Auckland, p.21.

3   Claire Matthews, *New Zealand Retirement Expenditure Guidelines*, NZ Fin-Ed Centre, Massey University, Auckland, p.5.
4   Lucy Swinnen, 'More than a Quarter of Women Accessing Wellington Boarding House Over 56', Stuff, 3 May 2017, www.stuff.co.nz/dominion-post/news/92009470/more-than-a-quarter-of-women-accessing-wellington-boarding-house-over-56 (accessed 20 September 2020).
5   New Zealand Government, 'Digital Inclusion and Wellbeing in New Zealand – Conclusions', www.digital.govt.nz/dmsdocument/161-digital-inclusion-and-wellbeing-in-new-zealand/html#conclusions (accessed 20 September 2020).
6   Holly Walker, *Alone Together: The Risks of Loneliness in Aotearoa New Zealand Following Covid-19 and How Public Policy Can Help*, The Helen Clark Foundation, Auckland, 2020, p.28.
7   Regular payments from family or friends that go towards food or bills can be treated as income by Work and Income, affecting any benefit a person receives.
8   M. Claire Dale and Susan St John, 'Gender: Pay & Pensions Gaps, and Penalty of COVID-19', RPRC PensionBriefing 2021-1, Retirement Policy and Research Centre, Business School, University of Auckland, 2021.

7. Digital Connection and Disconnection

1   Loneliness New Zealand Charitable Trust, 'Loneliness and Social Isolation Are Different', https://loneliness.org.nz/nz/facts/loneliness-and-social-isolation-are-different (accessed 10 August 2023).
2   Brian A. Primack, Ariel Shensa, Jaime E. Sidani, Erin O. Whaite, Liu Yi Lin, Daniel Rosen, Jason B. Colditz, Ana Radovic and Elizabeth Miller, 'Social Media Use and Perceived Social Isolation Among Young Adults in the US', *American Journal of Preventive Medicine*, 53, 1 (2017), pp.1–8.
3   Hadar Nesher Shoshan and Wilken Wehrt, 'Understanding "Zoom fatigue": A Mixed-Method Approach', *Applied Psychology*, 71, 3 (2022), pp.827–52.

Conclusion

1   Jean-Louis Guez de Balzac, *'Les Plaisirs de la Vie Retirée'*, *Dissertations Chrétiennes et Morales, 1665, XVIII.*

Acknowledgements

Thank you firstly to Tom Pearce; for everything, all the time.

Many thanks to Helen Clark and Peter Davis for their commitment to The Helen Clark Foundation, and the opportunity it provided us to undertake this research, and to WSP New Zealand who supported Holly's position at the Foundation.

Thank you also to David Kidd, for his suggestion that we look into loneliness, and to Max Harris for his editing advice. And finally thank you to BWB and the many people who have worked with us to turn this book into a small but mighty essay collection!

Kathy Errington
September 2023

About the Authors

Kathy Errington was the Founding Executive Director of the Helen Clark Foundation think tank from 2019 to 2023 and currently serves as the Deputy Director of the New Zealand Ministry of Foreign Affairs and Trade (MFAT) in Auckland. Her writing has appeared across national media outlets, including the *New Zealand Herald*, Newsroom and the *Sunday Star-Times*, and in the 2020 book *Shouting Zeros and Ones* (BWB).

Luke Fitzmaurice-Brown (Te Aupōuri) is a lecturer in law at Te Herenga Waka – Victoria University of Wellington, having previously completed his PhD at the University of Otago. Luke's research and teaching interests are centred on Te Tiriti o Waitangi, family law, child protection and children's rights.

Gaayathri Nair is a trained counsellor based in Wellington, and a current PhD candidate in public health at the University of Auckland. She has previously worked at Arohata women's prison as a counsellor.

Max Rashbrooke is a Wellington-based writer and public intellectual, with twin interests in economic inequality and democratic renewal. His latest book is *Too Much Money: How Wealth Disparities Are Unbalancing Aotearoa New Zealand* (BWB, 2021), based on research he carried out as the 2020 JD Stout Fellow at Victoria University of Wellington. A senior associate of the Institute for Governance and Policy Studies, he writes a fortnightly column for Stuff, and his work appears in outlets such as the *Guardian* and *Prospect* magazine. His TED Talk on upgrading democracy has been viewed over one million times.

Carrie Stoddart-Smith (Ngāpuhi, Ngāti Whātua) is a Principal Trade and Economies Consultant at OpinioNative Aotearoa, a consultancy she founded in January 2020, to honour Indigenous knowledge by creating an environment that celebrates and liberates Indigenous voices globally. She ran for the Māori Party in the electorate of Pakuranga in the 2017 general election.

Susan Strongman is an experienced journalist and communications specialist with a demonstrated history of work across print, radio and visual media. She has previously worked at Radio New Zealand and the *New Zealand Herald*.

Kiki Van Newtown is the parent of two kids, raising them on a diet of hashbrowns, soysages and feminist discourse in the upper Lower Hutt. Kiki performs with her partner, Jason, in their band Giantess.

Holly Walker has been working at the interface of politics, policy and advocacy for more than a decade. She is currently the Manager of Environment and Emissions Strategy at the Ministry of Transport, and she was Deputy Director at The Helen Clark Foundation from 2020 to 2022. Her BWB Text *The Whole Intimate Mess* was published in 2017. Holly Walker holds a PhD in Creative Writing from the International Institute of Modern Letters at Victoria University of Wellington. She is also a former Green Party MP.

Athena Zhu is an entrepreneur and business executive. She spent over a decade overseas, working for the Boston Consulting Group and Heineken, and founded a venture capital backed start-up that serves vegan dairy alternatives in China. Originally trained as an engineer, she is now studying counselling at Waikato University after returning to Aotearoa in 2022 with her husband.

About BWB Texts

BWB Texts are short books on big subjects for Aotearoa New Zealand. Over 100 Texts have been published since the series launched in 2013, available in print and digital formats. These can be purchased from all good bookstores and online from www.bwb.co.nz. To celebrate the milestone of publishing 100 Texts, starting from the 101st Text, each new title will feature its sequential number on the front cover.

BWB Texts include:

Abolishing the Military: Arguments and Alternatives
Griffin Manawaroa Leonard, Joseph Llewellyn and Richard Jackson

Encounters Across Time
Judith Binney

Introducing The Women's Suffrage Petition
Edited by Jared Davidson, historical essay by Barbara Brookes

Introducing Te Tiriti o Waitangi
Edited by Jared Davidson, historical essay by Claudia Orange

Introducing He Whakaputanga: He Tohu Series
Edited by Jared Davidson, historical essay by Vincent O'Malley

Privilege in Perpetuity: Exploding a Pākehā Myth
Peter Meihana

The Best of E-Tangata, Volume Two
Tapu Misa and Gary Wilson (eds)

More Zeros and Ones: Digital Technology, Maintenance and Equity in Aotearoa New Zealand
Anna Pendergrast and Kelly Pendergrast (eds)